How to Plan a

Wedding

A Roadmap to Guide You
from Engagement to "I Do"

Risa J. Weaver-Enion

Dear Hailey —
I hope you find this book
useful as you plan your wedding!
Best, Dgm

First edition 2021

www.risajamesevents.com
risa@risajamesevents.com

ISBN: 978-1-7377986-0-6 paperback
978-1-7377986-1-3 ebook

Author photo by Stacey Doyle Photography
Cover artwork by Matt Dull

Design and publishing assistance by The Happy Self-Publisher

Printed in the United States of America

For my husband, Rhead, who encouraged
me to start my own business, and who has been
endlessly supportive ever since.

Contents

Introduction

Welcome! Allow me to be the 4,325th person to say, "Congratulations on your engagement!" It never gets old, does it? Being engaged is an exciting time. But it can also be a stressful time if you're feeling overwhelmed by wedding planning.

Whether you've been day-dreaming about your wedding day since you were a kid, or you haven't put any thought into it whatsoever, planning a wedding is a BIG DEAL. You'll have to hire a team of wedding professionals to cover all aspects of the day: prep, photography, food and drink, music and entertainment, decor, attire…the list goes on. You'll have to think about things that aren't part of a normal person's day-to-day life. You'll be spending a lot of money on just one day, and you want to be sure you don't make any mistakes.

That's where I come in.

As a professional wedding planner, I have years of experience helping couples plan weddings, and I have advice on every wedding-related topic out there. But not everyone can afford to hire a full-service wedding planner, so I decided to write this book to share my experience and knowledge with as many people as possible. People like you!

There are so many decisions to be made when it comes to a wedding that it can be hard to know where to start. And once you start making a list, it can get overwhelming pretty quickly. I'm going to walk you through the entire wedding planning process, step-by-step, so you always know how to make the right decision and what you should focus on next.

This book begins with a few places to find wedding inspiration. Chances are you're already familiar with some of these, but I tried to include a few more obscure and esoteric sources. Most of them are online sources because that's the world we live in now.

Next I cover the not-very-sexy-but-absolutely-essential topic of budgeting. Wedding costs can add up fast. Those gorgeous weddings you see photos of on Pinterest might be unrealistically expensive. Once you start researching service providers (such as caterers, photographers, and DJs), you won't know whether you can afford a particular one unless you've created a budget first. The Budget chapter includes worksheets and templates that you can use to bring order to chaos.

Once we get the dollars under control, it's time to start thinking big picture: what do you want your wedding day to look like? Design is the really fun part, where you let your imagination run wild (and pull out those Pinterest boards you've been stocking with pretty images) to figure out what your goals are.

The next chapter of the book is Hiring Wedding Pros. I break down for you what goes into choosing each of the many service providers who will work together to make your wedding day beautiful.

The Details chapter covers exactly what it says it will: all the little details like attire, gifts, signage, songs, and more. There's a saying, "Life is in the details." That couldn't be more true for a wedding. But don't worry. I've thought of all the details so you don't have to.

At the end of each section is a link to a questionnaire you can use when interviewing prospective wedding service providers. Each questionnaire contains a list of relevant questions for each category of service to help you find the right fit.

This book is proudly LGBTQ+ friendly and provides tips and advice for same-sex as well as opposite-sex couples. The wedding industry, unfortunately, can be hetero-normative and cisgender-focused, but LGBTQ+ couples can feel comfortable in this space and welcomed by this book and by me.

Whether you have 15 weeks or 15 months to plan your wedding, this book will help you cut through all the noise and bring clarity to your planning process. Follow the steps I give you, and you will have a joyful and well-organized wedding planning experience!

How to Use This Book

This book is meant to be a roadmap for planning your wedding. The chapters are organized in the order in which you should think and plan. At the end of each section, there's a homework assignment for you to complete. You will have more success planning your wedding if you complete each homework assignment before moving on to the next section.

If you have a year or more in which to plan your wedding, it could be helpful for you to read the book all the way through once, without completing the homework assignments. That way you'll get a bird's-eye overview of the entire planning process. After that, you can read the book a second time and complete the homework assignments at the end of each section.

Much of this homework is intended to be done by you as a couple. Even if one of you is shouldering more of the planning responsibilities, you're both getting married, so you should both have some input into the final event.

Do yourself a favor, and set up a dedicated wedding email address right now, before you begin reading. Use this email address for all wedding business to easily keep track of things. And make sure both partners have access to the email address.

Happy reading!

CHAPTER 1

Finding Inspiration

Sources of Inspiration

Wedding Magazines

Wedding magazines aren't quite as prevalent as they once were, thanks to the rise of the Internet and social media. Blogs now fill the role that magazines once played. But you can still find a handful of wedding titles on the magazine stand. Look for *Martha Stewart Weddings*, *BRIDE's*, *Inside Weddings*, and *Modern Bride*.

Local wedding publications can be even more helpful than the national brands. One of the problems with reading the national publications is that the real weddings featured are often in destination locales. It doesn't help you to know which Italian wedding professionals put together a fabulous wedding if you live in Baltimore.

The Knot digitally publishes several regional versions of its magazine, which is full of information about wedding service providers who are actually in your area. If you Google the name of your city or state plus "wedding magazine," chances are that something helpful will come up.

Wedding Blogs

The rise of wedding blog *Style Me Pretty* in the late 2000s launched a plethora of similar blogs where you can find all sorts of inspiration. Be warned, most of these blogs still predominantly feature white, heterosexual, cis-gender couples.

Here's a list of some of the most well-known wedding blogs:

- Style Me Pretty
- Junebug Weddings
- Ruffled Blog
- Bridal Musings
- Wedding Chicks
- Green Wedding Shoes

- Grey Likes Weddings
- 100 Layer Cake

For LGBTQ+ wedding inspiration, try:

- Equally Wed
- Gay Weddings & Marriage Magazine
- Men's Vows
- Pridezillas
- Mrster

And here are some other specialty blogs:

- Pretty Pear Bride
- Perfête
- Amor Latino Unveiled
- Latino Bride & Groom
- Weddings of Color

Note that blogs are constantly coming and going, so it's possible that some of these will have shut down by the time you read this. Google is always your best friend when it comes to finding resources for wedding planning.

Social Media Accounts

Most, if not all, of the blogs listed above also have social media accounts. As I will say approximately 1 million times in this book, Instagram and Pinterest are the two biggest sources for all things wedding. Instagram is better for connecting with wedding pros, and Pinterest is better for inspiration. Use them both wisely and you will have no shortage of ideas for your wedding!

Many wedding pros tag the entire wedding team in their social media posts, so if you follow a few local wedding pros, you may soon get a sense for the wedding community in your area.

Now, let's move on to what might be the hardest part of planning a wedding: creating a budget.

CHAPTER 2

Budget

Links to Templates

To help you manage your budget and your guest list, I've created spreadsheet templates. I used these templates for my own wedding, and I use them for my clients to this day. You'll need these templates to complete the first few homework assignments.

The templates are set up as Google Sheets workbooks. To use them, click on the link below or type the URL into your browser bar to open the master copy, which is set to "View Only."

From the main menu bar, select "File" then "Make a copy." Save this copy to your own Google Drive account, and then make entries and changes as needed.

The Budget Template

The Budget template has a main sheet where you can enter your overall budget in the blue box at the top. It will then auto-populate the dollar amounts allocated to each main category. These dollar amounts are based on pre-set percentages. You can change the percentages to better suit your tastes and needs. The dollar amounts will automatically adjust when you change the percentage.

Each category has its own separate sheet, which is where you will enter your expenses as you incur them. Entries on the sub-sheets will auto-populate onto the main sheet. This allows you to see at a glance how much money you've spent or committed to spend and how much remains of your original budget.

Find the Budget Template at bit.ly/RJE-budget

The Guest List Template

The Guest List template is more than just a place to list names. It also has columns for number of guests, addresses, and information you will need to keep track of throughout the planning process.

If you are serving a pre-plated meal (as opposed to a buffet), you will need to track guests' meal selections as you receive their response cards back. You can also use the guest list template to track when you sent a save-the-date, when you sent an invitation, whether you've received a response, how many are attending, special dietary needs, what type of gifts you received (shower or wedding), and whether you sent a thank you note yet.

Column A is labeled "Number" for a specific reason—DO NOT DELETE THIS COLUMN. Even though the spreadsheet automatically includes line numbers for all sheets, you want to assign a separate number to each invitation. This allows you to sort and re-sort the spreadsheet, and the assigned number will travel with the party's name.

The reason you want to assign a number to each invitation is simple: some people will return their response card and forget to fill out their name!

Before you mail the invitations, write on the back of each response card (in pencil, somewhere discreet, like the corner) the number that corresponds with that invitation. That way, if you get back a response card with no name on it, you can cross-reference the number on the back with your master list and figure out who the card belongs to. If you manage and receive RSVPs via your wedding website, you won't have to worry about this.

Feel free to create your own additional tabs in this spreadsheet to create invitation lists for showers, bachelor/bachelorette parties, the rehearsal dinner, and any post-wedding events, like a brunch.

Find the Guest List Template at bit.ly/RJE-guest-list

Where Is the Money Coming From?

The first rule of planning a wedding is: Never go into debt for your wedding. If you can't afford the wedding that you want, you should either hold off until you can save more money or you should revise your plans. It's just not worth going into debt.

Credit Cards—Just Don't Do It

If you want to use credit cards to earn points, be sure you can afford to pay the balance in full each month.

Payment apps like Venmo will allow you to pay with a credit card (and most wedding pros accept payment by app these days), but the apps charge a fee to use a credit card (usually 3%). No matter how many points your credit card company is giving you, they won't be enough to justify the additional 3%. (If you don't believe me, spend a little time on The Points Guy's website.)

Budget for What You Can Afford

So if you're not going into debt to fund your wedding, where is the money going to come from? There are really only four options: your current income, your savings, your investments, or family (usually parent) contributions.

How to Ask Parents for Financial Assistance

Putting together your wedding budget might involve some uncomfortable conversations with your parents, but it's better to get them out of the way now. Don't frame the conversation as if you expect money from them. "Are you able to contribute something to our wedding fund?" is a better question than, "How much can you contribute to our wedding fund?"

Traditionally, the bride's family paid for the wedding, and the groom's family paid for the rehearsal dinner (and sometimes the bar tab for the wedding). Things are much less cut-and-dried these days. Many more women have jobs than in previous generations. Many couples are waiting until they are older and more established financially before getting married. And LGBTQ+ couples don't fit into those out-dated gender roles. If both sets of parents are contributing to the wedding fund, it can be easier to put all the money in one basket and allocate it as needed, rather than designating money from one set of parents as only for the rehearsal dinner.

When asking either set of parents for money, you should keep in mind one important thing: anyone who contributes money gets a say in how that money is spent. If you are afraid that your mom will object to your ideas and try to turn it into "her" wedding instead of your wedding, then you might be better off turning down her money. Similarly, if you envision an intimate wedding with just family and your closest friends, you might be surprised that your prospective father-in-law wants to invite his 20 best clients to the wedding. If he contributes money to the wedding, he gets more of a say in the guest list. It's the original Golden Rule: He who has the gold, makes the rules.

How To Allocate Your Total Budget Amount

Once you know your total amount of available funds, it's time to start breaking it down into categories. Broadly speaking, there are four major categories of spending:

1. attire and preparation
2. ceremony
3. reception
4. details

You'll notice what's not included there—rings and a honeymoon. Those items are typically considered to be outside of the wedding budget.

Usually the engagement ring has already been purchased before a wedding budget even takes form, and wedding bands are considered gifts from one spouse to the other. Each person is responsible for buying his or her fiancé(e)'s band.

As for the honeymoon, not everyone takes one. Some couples decide to delay their honeymoon, either because they can't take time off work for both the wedding and the honeymoon or because they want more time to save money for the honeymoon. As we work through the remainder of the budgeting chapter, just remember that if you want to use some of your wedding fund for the honeymoon, you'll have to cut back in all the wedding categories.

So let's get granular!

Your Homework Assignment

Open the Budget Worksheet that comes with this book (reminder: it can be found here bit.ly/RJE-budget). Use the "Worksheet" tab to enter the following amounts.

1. Check your bank statements and tally up the total amount of money you have on hand right now to allocate toward your wedding budget. (Hint: this should not be all of your money. You still need some savings for emergencies.)

2. Ask your parents if they are able to contribute to your wedding budget, and if so, how much.

3. Analyze your current monthly income and household expenses and determine whether you can reasonably set aside a certain amount per month to go toward wedding expenses. Add that to your total budget amount.

Pour yourself a drink. You'll need it for the next section.

Wedding Budget Categories

As you'll recall from the previous section, there are four broad categories for any wedding:

1. attire and preparation
2. ceremony
3. reception
4. details

Let's break down those categories into their sub-parts. Keep in mind that these breakdowns are meant to be overly inclusive. You may or may not need some of these items. And some items are included with other items. For example, when you hire a DJ for your reception, typically they will also handle music for your ceremony, and appropriate microphones will be part of the package. Similarly, I've listed "photography" and "videography" under both Ceremony and Reception, but those service providers will be handling both the ceremony and the reception.

Attire & Preparation

(for a bride and groom; adjust as necessary for LGBTQ+ couples)

- Bride
  - Wedding gown
  - Shoes
  - Veil
  - Tiara or other hair accessory
  - Undergarments (bra, underwear, hosiery, underskirts, garter)
  - Jewelry (earrings, necklace, bracelet)
  - Handbag or clutch
  - Rehearsal dinner dress and shoes
  - Bridal shower dress and shoes
  - Hair stylist (including a trial)
  - Makeup artist (including a trial)
  - Manicure/Pedicure

- Groom
  - Tuxedo, suit, or other coordinated outfit (rented or purchased)
  - Shoes (rented or purchased)
  - Tie and pocket square
  - Socks/other undergarments
  - Cufflinks (and button covers for a tuxedo)
  - Rehearsal dinner suit and shoes
  - Haircut
  - Men's manicure
- Wedding Party Attendants
  - Accessories (often the groomsmen are given a tie and pocket square as a gift, and the bridesmaids are given jewelry or pashminas)
  - Hair stylist (if you are requiring professional hair styling, it's customary to pay for it)
  - Makeup artist (same as for hair)

Ceremony

- Site fee
- Officiant fee
- Musicians (either the same as for the reception, or ceremony-only live music)
- Floral décor (arch, aisle or chair décor, altar arrangements)
- Bouquets, boutonnières, and corsages (known as "personal flowers")
- Flower girl and ring bearer accessories (fresh flower petals, baskets, pillows, etc.)
- Photography
- Videography
- Coordinator
- Chair rental
- Aisle runner
- Microphone rental

Reception

- Venue rental
- Table, chair, and linen rental

- Tableware rental (plates, glasses, flatware, napkins)
- Lounge area furniture rental
- Food and beverages
- Cake or other desserts
- Staffing (bar, chefs, servers, security)
- Floral décor (centerpieces, accent arrangements, sweetheart table)
- Lighting and draping
- Music or entertainment
- Photography
- Videography
- Coordinator

Details

- Gifts for parents
- Gifts for wedding party (see Wedding Party Accessories above)
- Favors for guests
- Stationery (save-the-dates, invitations, RSVP cards, inserts, programs, escort cards or seating chart, place cards, menus, thank you notes)
- Postage (for save-the-dates, invitations, RSVP cards, and thank you notes)
- Signage (directional, welcome, guest book, cards/gifts, unplugged ceremony, bar, desserts, favors, sparklers, etc.)
- Calligraphy
- Guest book and pens
- Card box
- Personalized Champagne flutes
- Engraved cake cutting set
- Garter
- Table numbers
- Welcome bags for out-of-town guests
- Transportation (for yourselves, the wedding party, and/or your guests)
- Valet parking attendants
- Event insurance
- Gratuities

Percentage Breakdown

When it comes to the budget, it can be helpful to start by thinking in percentage terms. Here's a sample breakdown of how much to allocate to the major components of a wedding:

50%	ceremony and reception (including officiant fee, site fees, food, and beverage)
10%	photography and videography
10%	floral and décor (table arrangements, ceremony décor, personal flowers, rental items, linens, lighting, drapery)
10%	attire and beauty
5%	music/entertainment (for both ceremony and reception)
5%	planner or coordinator
2.5%	favors and gifts (for spouse-to-be, parents, attendants, and guests)
2.5%	transportation
2.5%	cake or desserts
2.5%	stationery and postage

Sample Budget

If you have a total budget of $40,000, here's what that looks like by category:

$20,000	officiant fee, site fees, food, and beverage
$4,000	photography and videography
$4,000	all floral and décor
$4,000	all attire and beauty
$2,000	entertainment
$2,000	planner or coordinator
$1,000	favors and gifts
$1,000	transportation
$1,000	cake or desserts
$1,000	stationery and postage

This gives you a benchmark to work with when you start researching venues and wedding pros. If you find a photographer who charges $10,000 for weddings, then you know they are out of your budget and you should move on.

You also know that if you decide to splurge in a category, then you need to reduce a different category by the same amount in order to stay on-budget. Conversely, if you spend less than your budget in a particular category, you can either apply the extra money to a different category, or just consider it savings.

A Note About Having a Wedding Coordinator

I know you bought this book because you want to plan your own wedding. But there is a difference between planning your own wedding and coordinating your own wedding. We'll dive into this in more detail in Chapter 4, but I cannot stress enough that you will need to hire a professional to execute your wedding day.

Once you've made all the decisions and hired a pro team, you will still need a professional wedding coordinator to put together a wedding timeline for you and to be with you on your wedding day to make everything run smoothly. You will be far too busy having fun to coordinate your own wedding, as will your family and friends. It's not possible to be a guest at a wedding and be the coordinator at a wedding. If you want your wedding to be a success, you need a wedding coordinator, so please include that in your budget from the beginning.

Your Homework Assignment

Enter your overall budget amount from the previous section into the box on the "Total Budget" tab of the Budget Worksheet. The category breakdowns will automatically populate based on my pre-determined percentages.

Make adjustments based on your personal preferences. For example, if a raging dance party with a band is more important to you than flowers, reduce the percentage in the Floral and Décor category and increase by the same amount the Entertainment category.

Drafting a Guest List

During the early days of your engagement, you'll be thinking about your wedding guest list and whom to invite. You can't really start venue shopping until you know roughly how many people will attend your wedding. You also need to keep your budget in mind when booking a venue or any service professionals, and guest count is the single greatest driver of the cost of your wedding.

Guest Count Drives Overall Expense

Think about it: the more people you have, the more food you need. The more drinks you need. The larger a cake you need. You need more tables and chairs, and centerpieces to go on those tables. You need more take-home favors, if you're doing them. You might even need more aisle décor if you're going to have 10 or 12 rows of chairs versus 4 rows of chairs.

A high guest count can also limit your venue options. Many venues are not designed for more than 200 guests. And if your guest count gets into the 400–500 range, you might have only one or two options in your area.

So managing your guest count from the beginning is key!

When you begin putting together your guest list, start big and whittle down. Put everyone you think you might want to invite on a list. You can always cut later if you need to. This is also the time to ask both sets of parents for the names of guests they would like to invite.

Remember what I said about budgeting: if your parents are contributing financially, they also get to invite guests. If you want complete control over your guest list, you either need to pay for the entire wedding yourself, or hope that your parents and future in-laws don't want to invite anyone.

Even if parents are not contributing financially, they may want to include certain family members or close friends. Have a conversation with them up front to avoid hurt feelings later.

Who Should Be Included?

How do you decide who should be on your guest list? There are three basic categories into which your invitees will fall: family, friends, and colleagues. These categories can be further broken down into sub-categories. We'll tackle family first.

Family

Obviously parents and siblings should be included in your guest list (unless there are family rifts; every family has its own dynamics). Generally, grandparents, aunts, uncles, and cousins are also automatic invitees.

Extended family is a little trickier. Great-aunts and -uncles. Second cousins. First cousins once removed. In-laws of your immediate family. Things can get a little complicated if there are divorces and remarriages, resulting in step-siblings you didn't grow up with, step-cousins, or other, tenuous relations.

Here, you have to make decisions based on your personal situation. Do you know these people? How often do you see them? If they didn't invite you to their wedding, would you be offended? Put them on the master list, and mark them as potential cuts for later.

Usually your parents are going to be the ones inflating the family category and insisting that you have to invite great-aunt Susie, even though you're not sure you know who great-aunt Susie is. Here are a few guidelines for you:

- People you've never met do not need to be at your wedding.
- People you haven't seen since you were a toddler probably don't need to be at your wedding.
- People you don't like definitely don't need to be at your wedding.

You may have to have some tough conversations with your parents about this, but just tell them you heard it from a pro.

Oh, and in case you're wondering, it's your responsibility to have those tough conversations with your parents, and it's your future spouse's responsibility to have the conversations with their parents.

Friends

Once you've gotten all the family members accounted for, you can move on to friends. This is a huge category! You've got your friends, your partner's friends, your joint friends, your parents' friends, and your partner's parents' friends. This is usually where guest lists go off the rails.

Your and Your Partner's Friends

It might be helpful to start with childhood friends and work your way up chronologically to the present. If you haven't seen someone in years, maybe they don't need to be at your wedding. If someone has never met your fiancé(e), then they potentially don't need to be at your wedding, but this is more of a grey area.

People you regularly socialize with will likely expect to be invited to your wedding, and you clearly like them, otherwise you wouldn't be socializing with them, so they should be an easy add.

It can be helpful to choose a cut-off date by which to judge these friendships. For example, if you haven't seen a particular friend in five or more years, they probably don't really need to be at your wedding. If you and your fiancé(e) have been dating for any length of time (more than a couple of years) and they still haven't met him or her (or their friends haven't met you), then they probably don't need to be at your wedding.

Always remember this: your wedding is the beginning of your life together as a married couple. It's a celebration of you AS A COUPLE. Your guest list should mostly consist of people who know you as a couple.

Parents' Friends

Friends of parents is a trickier category, mainly because it involves the judgment of your parents and your future in-laws. Start here: have you ever met these people? No matter how close they are to your parents, no one should have to be surrounded by strangers on their wedding day. People you've never met are a hard pass.

If your parents are members of a country club, or something similar, they probably have a large circle of friends "from the club." And depending on the club (and the friends) their children's weddings might be their way of "showing off" to their friends. Don't get caught up in this game.

Remember the prime directive from above: the wedding is a celebration of your love and the beginning of your married life. It's not a status symbol, and it's not an opportunity for your parents to show off to their friends.

Colleagues

Work colleagues are a hornet's nest. Again, there are many sub-categories to think about because you and your fiancé(e) each have work colleagues, and so do all of your parents.

Your and Your Partner's Colleagues

If you have colleagues with whom you regularly socialize outside of work, then there is good reason to invite them to your wedding. If you are close to your boss and would not feel at all uncomfortable having them see you drinking and dancing (as you are likely to do at your own wedding), feel free to add them to the list. By no means are you obligated to invite your boss, or anyone else.

It can be difficult to invite just one or two people from work without ending up inviting a whole bunch of people from work. Do you really want to feel like you're at work on your wedding day? Probably not.

If you are close to one or two colleagues but don't want to invite the whole office or your entire team, simply ask those you invite to keep the invitation to themselves. And you should limit the amount of time you spend talking about your wedding at work. (You should do this anyway, but especially if you aren't inviting a lot of colleagues.)

Parents' Colleagues

When it comes to colleagues of parents, it's best to rule them out. Chances are, you don't know these people, have never met these people, and have only heard about them from stories your parents tell. They don't need to be at your wedding.

Your parents might think these colleagues need to be at your wedding, but your parents are wrong. Your parents will be busy with parental wedding duties and catching up with family (and possibly their close friends who made the cut). Adding work colleagues to the mix just means you're buying dinner for a bunch of people who don't know anyone but your parents and maybe a couple of other work colleagues.

If your parents play the money card in order to invite more people, counter with the fact that you definitely appreciate their financial contribution, but you would rather put it toward the overall cost of the wedding (maybe serve a more expensive entrée, or get the floral décor you really want but is expensive) than invite people you don't know to the biggest day of your life.

But hey, if money is no object, ignore everything I wrote above and invite everyone you've ever met!

Exes

Ex-romantic partners are even more of a hornet's nest than work colleagues. This is a very sticky situation that is best handled on a case-by-case basis between you and your fiancé(e). If you are legitimately friends with an ex, and your fiancé(e) has met them and is fine with it, then by all means invite them. But I cannot stress enough how important it is for this to be a joint decision between you and your partner.

Who Gets a "Plus-One"?

Even after you finish the first pass at putting together your guest list, you still aren't finished. The next step is to figure out which people on your list should be invited as a pair. Colloquially, who gets a plus-one?

Married Couples & Engaged Couples

Couples that are either married or engaged MUST be invited as a pair. They are a social unit, and it's simply unacceptable to invite one without the other. (Even if you did, they most likely wouldn't attend without their partner.)

But what if one of your friends is married to a guy you don't like? Too bad! You have to invite them together or not at all. And to be honest, you'll barely notice that the guy is even there. You will be busy on your wedding day. You don't get to spend a significant amount of time with anyone except your wedding party and your new spouse. So if your friend has to bring her annoying husband, just let it be.

Couples Who Live Together

Much like married and engaged couples, couples who live together have made a commitment to each other and should be considered a social unit. Some cohabitating couples have no intention of ever getting married, but they are a team and should be treated as such.

Couples in a Long-Term Relationship

In these cases, things get slightly trickier. It's always polite to include a person's partner in any social invitation. If you have the budget for it, you should invite long-term couples as a pair, even if you only know one half of the couple. My advice to clients is that anyone dating for more than one year should be considered long-term.

If you decide to invite only the half of the couple that you know, then you should be prepared for that person to decline the invitation. So if it's someone important to you, go ahead and include their partner.

People Casually Dating or Singletons

You should feel no obligation to give your less-attached friends and family a plus-one. But again, it would be the gracious thing to do if your budget allows. Most people like to attend social events with someone, whether a date or a friend, especially if they won't know anyone other than the couple getting married.

Avoid "& Guest"

Regardless of which category your guests fall into, try to track down names for everyone. No one likes to be relegated to "& Guest." You will likely have to reach out to some people for their addresses anyway, which is also the perfect time to find out the name (first & last) of their significant other. The exception to this is people who are single. At the time invitations go out, they likely won't know who they might bring with them. But ideally they will put the guest's name on the response card, because you'll need it later for escort cards or a seating chart.

Children as Guests

As you are drafting your guest list, you also have to decide whether or not to include children.

When it comes to children at weddings, you essentially have three options: 1) include all children, 2) exclude all children, or 3) include only a select few children, usually either immediate family or wedding party members.

If you choose option 2 or 3, you need to let your guests know that children are not invited. So how do you convey to your guests that you're having an adults-only wedding?

How to Convey a "No Children" Guest List Policy

Traditionally, there was an easy, if subtle, way to let guests know that children were not invited to a wedding: you left their names off the invitation. The outer envelope of a wedding invitation would be addressed to "Mr. & Mrs. First Name Last Name" and the inner envelope would be addressed with their first names. This indicated that only the people named were invited to the wedding.

But these days, people don't know or follow proper etiquette rules, so addressing an invitation to only the adults isn't sufficient to indicate that children aren't invited. (Not to mention that many people have done away with the whole "outer envelope/inner envelope" wedding invitation system.)

Word-of-Mouth

You can begin letting guests know that children aren't invited when you talk to them about your wedding. Chances are that if you're inviting someone to your wedding, you know them well enough to know whether or not they have children. If they do, when you have conversations with them about your wedding, you can work into the conversation that you're having an adults-only wedding.

Say something like, "Let me know if you need local babysitting recommendations. We really want to celebrate with you at our wedding, but we're having an adults-only party." You're making sure they know you want them there, and you're trying to be helpful and sensitive to the fact that they have kids, but you're also making it clear that their kids aren't invited.

Your Wedding Website

Your wedding website is intended to be a place where guests can go to find out information about your wedding. It makes perfect sense to include information about whether children are invited. You can do this on a Frequently Asked Questions tab, or just in the description of the event. Here's some sample language:

"As much as we love your children, our wedding will be adults only. Alcohol will be served and there will be no available childcare. For everyone's safety and enjoyment, we hope you'll be able to make other care arrangements for your children. We look forward to celebrating with you!"

Information about local childcare providers can also be included on your wedding website, or just a note to inquire with you if they need recommendations.

Your Wedding Invitation

This is a more subtle approach than putting it on your wedding website, but less subtle than the traditional approach. Somewhere on your actual wedding invitation, include the words "Adults-Only Reception" or "Adult Reception to Follow."

With this verbiage, it's possible that someone will bring their children to the ceremony with the intention of leaving before the reception begins. Or, if your ceremony is at a different location than the reception, they may take the kids home in between or have someone pick them up before the reception. This is highly dependent on the specifics of your wedding day and their situation.

How to Handle an RSVP with Uninvited Children

If someone fills out the RSVP card and includes their children, then you'll have to take a more direct approach. A phone call to let them know that children can't be accommodated at the wedding will hopefully do the trick. It's possible they'll have to decline the invitation if they can't bring their kids, so you should be prepared for that possibility. But don't make an exception unless you can justify it to everyone else who's going to want you to make an exception for them. This is where having a hard-and-fast rule about including only children of immediate family members comes in handy.

Children in Your Wedding Party

If you are having children in your wedding, as flower girls or ring bearers, by all means, let them attend the wedding reception if you would like them to be there. But have a plan in place. That means having coloring books and crayons (or other age-appropriate children's activities) on hand so they don't get bored. It also means arranging for kids' meals with your caterer. Not only will the kids' meals be cheaper, but the kids will be happier.

You also can have children in your wedding party who don't come to the reception. Having a friend or extended family member who's not attending the wedding (or only attending the ceremony) pick them up and take them home after the ceremony or cocktail hour is a great solution.

Babies at Weddings

Babies are easier than children. They don't need a chair because they can't sit up yet. They don't need a meal because they're probably either breast-feeding or taking a bottle. And they can't get into trouble because they're confined to a stroller, carrier, or baby-wearing wrap. (They can also sleep through the craziest stuff.)

If you have friends or family members who have infants and you want to make life easier for them, let them know in person that they are welcome to bring their infant to your wedding. Sure, they might have to duck out of the ceremony if the baby cries, and they probably won't be out on the dance floor until the party ends, but at least they'll be there to celebrate with you.

Your Homework Assignment

Pour yourself another drink. It's about to get real. Get out a large pad of paper or open a blank document or spreadsheet on your laptop. (We're not ready to use the Guest List Template included with this book just yet.)

Make a list of everyone you might possibly want to invite to your wedding, and number the names as you go. Don't forget to include yourselves and your potential wedding party members on this list. Ask each set of parents for their preferred guest list and add them to your master list.

Decide whether you want to include children or not. Decide whether you want to give your single friends plus-ones or not. Add them to the tally if necessary.

Set your ground rules for who gets an invitation based on the parameters outlined earlier in this section. Eliminate anyone who doesn't meet the requirements you set.

If the list is overwhelming, consider where you can make cuts. If you originally included children, you might now change your mind. This is where those hard conversations with your parents come in if you need to cut someone from their list. Remember: you talk with your parents, your future spouse talks with their parents.

Once you have what looks like a manageable list, celebrate momentarily, but don't start verbally inviting anyone just yet. You may still have to make cuts once you start booking your wedding team and spending money. But you've accomplished a lot so far, so take a moment to appreciate that!

Selecting your wedding party

As a sub-set of your guest list, you need to decide whether to have a wedding party, and whom to ask to be part of it. Traditionally, the bride has a maid of honor and several bridesmaids, and the groom has a best man and several groomsmen.

Wedding party members are there to support the couple getting married and help with wedding-related tasks. The maid of honor and best man typically take on more responsibilities than other wedding party members. For example, they usually plan bachelor/bachelorette parties and give a toast at the reception. Maids of honor also often plan a bridal shower.

Traditionally, if a married woman was serving as an honor attendant, she was referred to as "matron" of honor, rather than "maid" of honor. But that has such a patriarchal feel to it, most couples opt to call her a maid of honor regardless of her own marital status.

As with traditional rules about who pays for which parts of a wedding, same-sex marriage has mooted some wedding party traditions, and mixed-gender wedding parties are becoming more common. Some brides opt for a man of honor or a bridesman, while grooms can have a best woman or groomswoman. "Best person" is a gender-neutral way to designate the honor attendant. Some couples opt to have their dogs fill those roles.

There are no rules, and you should do what works best for your situation.

Wedding Party vs. Bridal Party

First things first: I don't use the term "bridal party." It's extremely exclusionary and implies that the bride is the only person having a wedding. There's a groom too! Or two grooms! Or two brides (in which case, you can call it a bridal party and still be on safe ground). I strive to always be inclusive, so I use the term wedding party.

How to Select Your Wedding Party Attendants

It's worth keeping in mind that a larger wedding party will mean more expenses for you. It's customary for the couple to purchase gifts for each of their attendants. More attendants obviously equals more gifts. And if you will be paying for professional hair and makeup services for the women in your wedding party, that budget line item will need to be much larger for 10 ladies than it would be for five.

You should also keep personality in mind when choosing your wedding party. The honor attendants (i.e., maid of honor and best man, or whatever designation you use) have a lot of responsibilities, and your other attendants are expected to help out where they can. So you want to choose responsible individuals. If your best friend has never arrived anywhere on time in her entire life, you probably don't want her to be your right-hand woman for your big day.

People NOT to Invite to be in Your Wedding Party

You want to ask friends who get along well with others to be part of your wedding party. As a group, you will all spend a good deal of time together. One rotten fish spoils the whole barrel. Here are examples of personality types that don't make good wedding party members. Remember, I've been planning weddings for a long time. I've seen all of these in real life, and it never ends well.

The Diva

You will naturally want to include your sister or best friend in your wedding party, but give some real thought to their personality first. Are they the type of person who always wants to be the center of attention? Do they crave the spotlight? If so, you might want to rethink asking them to stand beside you on what is supposed to be your special day.

This goes for guys too. The point of your wedding party attendants is for them to support you as you get married. If they are the kind of person who wants the focus on them and they don't know how to be supportive, then they don't belong in your wedding party, even if they are your blood relatives!

Drug & alcohol addicts

This is going to sound harsh, but you don't want people battling drug and/or alcohol addiction to be in your wedding. They are unreliable and cannot be counted on for support. This goes triple if they aren't seeking treatment or trying to control their addiction issues.

I once had clients who lost one of their groomsmen two days before their wedding because his mother had checked him into rehab. This is not what you need two days before your wedding.

I had another set of clients whose groomsman physically assaulted two people at the wedding after the bartender cut him off for being visibly intoxicated. Again, this is not what you want for your wedding.

Drug and alcohol addiction are serious issues with serious complications. You may love or care for these people, but that doesn't necessarily mean that they need to be in your wedding.

Those suffering from depression or anxiety

This is an even more sensitive subject than drug and alcohol addition. Many people suffer from depression and/or anxiety. And many of them are actively treating their conditions, whether with medication or other techniques. Some of those with depression and anxiety are NOT treating their condition, and I have no qualms about advising you to avoid asking those people to participate in your wedding. For those who are managing their illness, it's a trickier situation.

Depression and anxiety are unpredictable. People have good days and bad days, and they usually don't know or have any control over when those bad days are going to happen. What if your wedding day happens to be one of their bad days?

If you have a sibling or friend you'd like to ask to be in your wedding but you know they have depression or anxiety, I suggest that you have an honest conversation with them. Let them know that it would mean a lot to you for them to participate, but that you want them to do what's best for them and their mental health. Let them know what would be expected of them. Be specific! Don't just rely on the fact that "everyone knows" what a bridesmaid or groomsman is supposed to do. Talk with them about specific responsibilities and be honest.

Let them be honest with you too. Don't take it personally if they decline to be in your wedding party. Take it as a sign that they care about you and want what's best for you on your wedding day. It takes a lot of grace and self-awareness for someone to realize that it's best for them to NOT be in your wedding party. Perhaps a low-pressure role performing a reading during the ceremony would be a better fit. It's easy to cut that at the last minute if they're not able to attend. Talk to them about other ways they can support you on your wedding day that don't involve being a bridesmaid or groomsman.

The Penny Pincher

If you ask someone to be in your wedding and their response is that they'd love to, as long as it doesn't cost them too much, I urge you to gracefully rescind the invitation. Being a bridesmaid or groomsman is, unfortunately, an expensive prospect. (Usually more so for the ladies.)

- They have to buy or rent attire and shoes.
- Bridesmaids generally attend at least one bridal shower (possibly contributing to the cost of hosting a bridal shower).
- Anyone attending a bridal shower generally buys a shower gift.
- They have to attend (or help host) the bachelor or bachelorette party.
- They have to attend the wedding, which may involve travel expenses.

- They might have to pay to have their hair and makeup professionally done.
- And they're probably going to want to give the couple a wedding gift.

That adds up.

Even if you, as the couple getting married, try to limit the expenses of your wedding party as much as possible, if someone is really strapped for cash, they are going to quibble with every. little. thing. It's going to cause you stress, and it might drive a wedge between you and your friend.

Being asked to be a bridesmaid or groomsman is an honor, and most people will perform the task admirably. But you can save yourself a lot of trouble if you put some serious thought into your choices before you extend your wedding party invitations.

And if I've stressed you out too much, just remember that there's no rule that says you have to have a wedding party. You can have only honor attendants, or none at all. I've had more than one client who had no wedding party, and everything worked out just fine.

How to Invite People to be Part of Your Wedding Party

When it comes time to actually ask your relatives or friends to be in your wedding, a simple phone call (or in-person get-together if you live in the same town) will do. There is no shortage of ideas on the Internet about cute ways you can ask your friends to be in your wedding party. If you have unlimited funds for your wedding, then sure, go ahead and spend $500 on these items. But if you would rather spend that $500 on something else, don't feel like you have to stage an elaborate, "Will you be in my wedding?" proposal.

Your Homework Assignment

Choose your wedding party members and ask them to be with you on your special day.

Congratulations! You've finished the difficult groundwork. Now we can move onto the fun stuff: design!

CHAPTER 3

Design

Sustainability

It's not often discussed, but weddings are incredibly wasteful. At the end of the night, there's a lot of stuff that ends up in the garbage: programs, escort cards, table numbers, floral arrangements, paper napkins, plastic cups, uneaten food, half-eaten cake, unfinished drinks. The list goes on.

While it's probably impossible to have a zero-waste wedding, it's definitely possible to cut way down on the waste. Sustainability is a growing trend in weddings, especially among more environmentally conscious young Millennials and Gen Z-ers. There are a number of opportunities for you to reduce waste while planning your wedding.

Stationery & Paper Goods

Save-the-Dates

One of the first things you will do in the planning process is send save-the-dates to your family and friends (once you've secured a venue and date, of course). Save-the-dates are often something fun, like a refrigerator magnet, but they can easily be sent digitally. Paperless Post is a great option for sending pretty invites and announcements without using any paper.

If you want to get a little fancier and include envelope liners and digital calligraphy, you'll have to purchase "coins" to redeem for those features, but it's still significantly less expensive than sending paper announcements, and the carbon footprint is practically zero.

Wedding Invitations

I love paper wedding invitations. I love the heavy-weight paper, the embossing, the size, the detail. And I love receiving a hand-calligraphed wedding invitation in the mail. It announces itself as something special.

But wedding invitations are paper-intensive. There's the outer envelope, the inner envelope, the invitation, the response card, the response card envelope, perhaps a map or directions insert, and maybe a brunch invitation. It's a lot!

You can, of course, send an electronic wedding invitation just as easily as you can send an electronic save-the-date. If you're not (pardon the pun) wedded to tradition, you may want to go that route. Again, sites like Paperless Post make it easy to extend invitations and track RSVPs.

You could also take a hybrid approach by sending a paper invitation but collecting RSVPs online via your wedding website. This cuts down on paper usage because you don't need to print and mail a paper response card with envelope. (It has the added advantages of saving you money and being faster than guests mailing back their responses.)

If you want to send paper invitations but still be environmentally friendly, you can have them printed on recycled or biodegradable paper. Some companies will even print your wedding invitations on seed paper, which is exactly what it sounds like: paper with seeds embedded in it. The paper is plantable, and maybe your guests will get some pretty wildflowers out of it. Some companies, like Paper Culture, plant a tree after every order.

One potential downside to sending electronic invitations is that older guests may not have email addresses or Internet access and may not be able to receive or respond to a digital invitation But this likely will affect only a small number of your guests. A good work-around to this problem is to order a small number of paper invitations for older guests (or for keepsake purposes) but to use electronic invitations for the majority of your guest list.

Signage

There are several wedding stationery items that can be signs instead of individual cards, namely, programs and escort cards.

Ceremony programs are a way to let guests know who's in the wedding and roughly what will take place during the ceremony. Usually these are printed as individual cards or booklets and placed on each seat before the ceremony begins. It gives guests something to look at while they wait.

But the information can just as easily be conveyed with a large sign on an easel displayed near the back of the ceremony site, where guests will see it as they walk in. Etsy is full of templates for ceremony program signage, and your local FedEx store can handle printing the large-format sign for you. You'll want to print any signage on foam-core board, not poster board. Foam-core is two layers of poster board with foam in between them. It's much sturdier than poster board.

Individual, tented escort cards make a beautiful display. But if sustainability is your goal, then a large seating chart is the way to go. Again, Etsy has approximately 1 million seating chart templates available for download.

The job of escort cards or a seating chart is to tell guests which table they're sitting at, but not which seats is theirs. Even if you're not assigning seats, table assignments are still highly recommended. Guests will be more comfortable if they know they have a specific place to go, rather than trying to find someone to sit with (and having flashbacks to stressful middle school cafeteria situations).

If your guest list is 100 or less, you can break out the seating chart by table. Table 1: list of names. Table 2: list of names. Etc. But if you have more than 100 guests, it can be difficult to scan the entire seating chart for one name. In that case, I recommend making the seating chart alphabetical. A — B: list of names with table numbers next to the names. C — D: list of names with table numbers. You get the idea. This makes it so much easier for guests to find their table.

And while we're on the subject of assigned tables, keep in mind that your tables don't have to be numbered. They could be named instead, which would eliminate the need for paper table numbers. Possibilities include naming tables after wine varietals, or books from classic literature, or favorite movies.

The item for which the table is named could be the "table number." A bottle of Cabernet Sauvignon would be placed in the middle of the table, instead of a number 2 in a stand. This idea works better for smaller weddings with 10 or fewer tables; otherwise, it turns into a scavenger hunt, with guests wandering all over the place trying to find the table that has their book (or whatever) on it. But it's a fun way to cut down on paper while also injecting some of your and your fiancé(e)'s personalities into your wedding.

We'll talk more about seating charts and stationery later in Chapter 5.

Florals

Choose local florals

Did you know that most of the flowers you see in grocery stores and florist shops are grown in South America? They're the floral equivalent of factory-farmed chickens. Vast flower farms use armies of low-paid workers to harvest their flowers, which are bred to be hardy enough to withstand travel. This means they have almost no fragrance and bear little genetic resemblance to their floral ancestors.

These are not the flowers you want for your wedding.

You want locally grown flowers, if possible. But even if you don't live in an area known for flower production, if your florist sources flowers from within the U.S. instead of internationally, they'll be higher quality.

Not to mention that using local or nearby flowers cuts down on their carbon footprint. Just like with produce, if the flowers have to travel from

South America, they've produced more carbon emissions than if they traveled from California or Florida.

Ask your floral designer where they source their flowers, or hire one who grows their own flowers.

In-season florals

In keeping with choosing locally sourced flowers, in-season flowers will also boost your sustainability. For example, if you want peonies in November, they're not going to be in season anywhere in the U.S., which means they'll have to come from the Southern Hemisphere.

Peony season runs from late April to mid-June in the continental U.S. Alaska peony season is July through September. And in Australia, they bloom October through December (spring in the Southern Hemisphere). Those peonies are going to have a huge carbon footprint because of the many miles they have to travel. And they won't smell as fragrant as a peony grown in Pennsylvania and meant for use within a narrower geographic radius.

Make a Statement

Choosing a single statement bloom for your bouquet reduces the number of flowers you need. Sunflowers, calla lilies, dahlias, magnolias, ranunculuses, garden roses, and even artichokes in bloom (yes, artichokes!) look beautiful as a single stem.

Go Green

There are also a lot of "floral" options that aren't flowers. You can use green plants as ceremony décor, table centerpieces, and accent pieces. Those can be planted in the ground after the wedding, rather than being thrown away.

Similarly, potted herbs in groups make for an interesting (and fragrant) table centerpiece option, especially for an outdoor wedding. If you still really want flowers, potted orchids are a good choice. They're beautiful, and given the number of blooms on each plant, a little can go a long way.

Succulents are another great choice, and they even come in different shades of green and purple, so your look doesn't have to be monochromatic. They have the added advantage of not wilting in the summer heat and humidity.

Food as Art

Piles of citrus in gold vases or compote dishes make for a vibrant, reusable, and earth-friendly centerpiece. Citrus can also be stacked in tall glass cylindrical vases so that it's contained but still visible. Or use fall fruits such as pomegranates and figs for a darker, moodier color scheme.

Multi-task and Re-use

It's easy to have your centerpieces do double-duty. You can use small potted herbs or succulents as escort cards. A card with the guest's name and table number can be put in the pot, then the guests will take their plant to their table and all the plants together will form centerpieces. The plants can even serve a third purpose and be their take-home favor!

If you're using larger plants, orchids, or floral arrangements as centerpieces, have a plan for one guest at each table to take home a centerpiece. This is something that can be worked out with your planner and DJ. Either something can be placed under one plate at each table, and the person sitting at that spot gets the centerpiece. Or the DJ can make a game of it (if that's something you're okay with).

Donate

There are a number of organizations that will come to your wedding at the end of the night, pick up the floral arrangements, and deliver them to hospital rooms and homeless shelters to brighten an otherwise depressing space. This ensures that your wedding flowers will be enjoyed for at least several days after your wedding is over. To find a group in your area, simply Google "donate wedding flowers" and your city name.

Compost

No matter what happens with your florals—you take them home, you give them to guests, you donate them—encourage composting when the flowers have wilted and died. Many communities offer yard-waste pickup through the trash company, but even tossing the dead flowers out in your own yard under a tree or shrub will allow them to decompose and provide the soil with some nutrients.

Non-floral Décor

Décor isn't limited to just flowers. It's also the vases that hold the flowers, the ceremony arch, lounge seating areas, garlands, and tchotchkes that help personalize your wedding. Rent as much of this as you can. If an item can be used and re-used by multiple people, then the energy required to make that item in the first place is amortized over many uses, reducing the overall carbon footprint of the item.

If you really want to buy, go thrifting! Many antique shops have an assortment of mismatched vases, flatware, bud vases, china, and other objects that you may want to incorporate into your wedding décor. If you buy pre-owned items, you are once again extending their useful life and reducing their overall impact on the environment.

Finding a Sustainable Wedding Venue

When it comes to your wedding venue search, availability on your ideal date and capacity for your anticipated number of guests are two important factors. But if you're also concerned with having a sustainable wedding, here are three key factors to focus on.

Geographic Location

Will a lot of your guests have to travel long distances, either by car or by plane, to get to your wedding? Travel = carbon emissions = larger carbon footprint. The easiest way to reduce your wedding's carbon footprint is to cut down on the amount of travel people have to do.

If you and your spouse-to-be live in one place, but both of your families live somewhere else, consider having the wedding where the most people are.

Aesthetics

The prettier your venue is, the less you will have to bring in as far as florals and décor. If you want an outdoor location, consider a botanical garden or venue with a sweeping vista. You won't need to bring in nearly as many florals, which will save you money as well as reducing waste.

If you're searching for an indoor venue, think "old." Buildings that were built before World War II are more likely to be ornate. Post-war hotel ballrooms are generally quite spartan. They're often designed with conferences and conventions in mind, not weddings. But if you can find a hotel from the late 1800s or early 1900s, it's likely to have an ornate tray ceiling, gilded walls, and a parquet floor. All of these make the room feel luxurious without having to bring in loads of décor.

LEED Certification

Buildings that are LEED Certified have met a stringent set of environmental requirements, mostly having to do with energy use, including HVAC, water, and recycling. (LEED stands for "Leadership in Energy and Environmental Design.")

LEED Certification comes in four levels: Certified, Silver, Gold, and Platinum, with Platinum being the highest level. The requirements become more numerous and stringent as the levels increase. If sustainability is your key requirement in a wedding venue, look for one that is LEED Platinum.

LEED Certification is time-consuming and expensive, so buildings are proud to tout their certification. If you're looking at a venue and you can't tell whether or not it's LEED Certified, it's probably not. If it were, they would be shouting it from the rooftops.

Sustainable Wedding Catering

Regardless of whether your wedding catering is being handled by your venue or an outside caterer, there are a few things you can do to increase your wedding's overall sustainability score:

1. Choose a caterer who uses locally grown foods from suppliers using sustainable growing practices. If you're not sure, ask!

2. Choose in-season foods for your wedding. Caprese salad skewers are a popular appetizer choice (cherry tomato, mozzarella, basil), but tomatoes are only in season in the summer (in the Northern Hemisphere). Don't serve caprese in November.

3. Find out what happens with leftover food. Will it be boxed for the family to take home, or can it be donated to a food bank? (State laws and regulations also affect the answers to this question, so you'll need to inquire with your caterer.)

4. Rent real china plates, real stainless steel flatware, and real glasses. The energy usage required to clean those items is lower than the environmental impact of disposables. If you absolutely must use disposable, be sure to use compostable items.

5. Whether you or the bar service is procuring the alcohol for your wedding, buy large format bottles. For wine, that means magnums (1.5 liter bottles) and for liquor, that means 1.75 liter bottles (a "handle"). This cuts down on the number of empty bottles that need to be recycled at the end of the night.

6. When it comes to beer, kegs are your most sustainable option. Kegs are cleaned and re-used, resulting in very little waste. Unlike bottles or cans, which all have to be disposed of (and hopefully recycled).

7. When choosing your wines, look for wineries that use organic, sustainable, or biodynamic farming or wine-making practices. A little research on their websites should be sufficient. Much like with LEED Certification, wineries that use these practices are proud of them and generally tout them on their websites and even on their bottles.

8. And lastly, straws—everyone's bugaboo. Be sure the bartenders aren't using plastic straws or stirrers for cocktails. Only paper straws or bamboo stirrers and skewers should be used. (And try to ensure that the paper straws are bio-degradeable and that they are actually being composted or recycled at the end of the night. Otherwise, you're not accomplishing much.) When it comes to straws and stirrers, your best bet is to choose cocktails that don't require them in the first place.

Hire Local Wedding Pros

As with choosing a venue that doesn't require a lot of your guests to travel long distances, choosing service providers who don't have to travel far will also do the most to reduce your wedding's carbon footprint. Photographers are notorious for wanting to travel to shoot weddings. But if you live in Montana, there's no sense in hiring a photographer from California (or Europe!) to shoot your wedding. There are tons of talented wedding photographers in Montana, I assure you.

And it doesn't even have to be out-of-state travel to make an impact. If you can hire a wedding pro who's 10 miles away from your venue, rather than 60 miles away, it makes a difference in the overall sustainability of your wedding. It's not out of line for you to ask potential wedding team members how far away they are from your venue—and don't be afraid to tell them why you're asking.

Choose Wedding Jewelry Wisely

It begins with engagement-ring shopping. One way to up your sustainability score is to purchase heirloom jewelry from an antique shop or estate jeweler. By now, you're probably familiar with the term "blood diamond" and the sometimes questionable mining practices used by some of the large worldwide diamond conglomerates. By buying an heirloom or antique ring, you're not contributing to the on-going financing of wars, and the metals and gemstones have already been mined, so there's no additional mining required for your ring.

Another option is to purchase a ring through a company like Brilliant Earth, which is committed to sustainable mining practices and works with local collectives in countries where gemstones are mined to ensure that workers are paid a fair wage and that the proceeds are reinvested into the community. You can even custom design a ring with them if you want something truly original.

Rent, Don't Buy

When it comes to attire, renting is always the more sustainable option. Bridesmaids can take advantage of companies like Rent the Runway to find fashionable gowns, and they don't have to worry that the gown will sit in the back of their closet for the next decade before they finally toss it or donate it.

Even if your groomsmen aren't wearing tuxedos, these days suits can be rented just as easily. But everyone should own at least one good suit, so it might make sense for your guys to buy, if they don't already have a suit and need to level-up their wardrobe game.

Hire Group Transportation

Hiring a shuttle service to ferry guests between the hotels and the wedding venue saves a lot of carbon emissions because instead of dozens of individual vehicles, you have one large one. But talk to the transportation company about what happens with the shuttle during the downtime between dropping off at the venue and heading back to the hotel at the end of the night. If the shuttle is going to spend five or six hours idling so the driver can keep the air conditioning going, then you're undermining the entire premise.

Make a Donation

Instead of take-home favors, make a donation to your favorite charitable or environmental organization. Or purchase carbon offsets to counter-act the carbon emissions generated by your wedding.

Use Soy Candles

Candles on guest tables set a romantic mood, but traditional candles emit particulates into the air. Use clean-burning soy candles to cut down on pollution.

Beauty

Talk to your hairstylist and makeup artist about their products. Are they cruelty-free and sustainable? Do they contain organic ingredients? Ask these questions before you hire them. If you really want to work with them because of their talent, but their products don't meet your standards, ask if they'll consider using different products for your wedding.

Honeymoon Responsibly

There are more and more sustainability-minded resorts opening every day. If you're really committed to the cause, you can build a community-service activity into your honeymoon plans and give back to whichever local community you're visiting.

Your Homework Assignment

Make a note of any of the above items that especially appeal to you. Discuss with the relevant wedding professional.

Now that you have your budget and a guest list, it's time to start thinking about when to have your wedding and what it will look like. As with everything else, there are steps to follow. Let's dive in.

Choosing a time of year

You might think it's a piece of cake to choose a wedding date, but there are a lot of things to take into consideration.

Plan at Least One Year in Advance

A good rule of thumb is to give yourself at least one year to plan your wedding. You will have the most flexibility with booking wedding pros with that much lead time. Weddings can certainly be planned in under a year, but your options will be limited if you have less lead time.

I recommend that couples have conversations prior to getting engaged about when they might like to get married. If you want an autumn wedding, but you don't get engaged until February, you're going to have a hard time. You might end up having to wait almost two years to get married at that point, or choose a different time of year.

There Are Only So Many Saturdays in a Year

Decide whether you must have a Saturday wedding or if you would be okay with a Friday or Sunday wedding. There are only 52 Saturdays in a year. And once you take into account that most weddings happen between April and October, that's only 28 Saturdays. Those Saturdays go fast! Especially the ones in June and October, which are the two most popular months to get married, nationwide.

Consider Family Events

Is someone in one of your families celebrating a milestone birthday the year you want to get married? Will there be a big family get-together for that event? Do you want to avoid that weekend, or try to incorporate your wedding celebration into the same weekend?

Does your family (or some part of your family) take an annual vacation at the same time every year? Do you want to work around that vacation to ensure that they can come to your wedding?

Consider Work Schedules

What do you do for a living? Accountants probably don't want to get married in the spring during tax season. People who work in the wine industry probably want to avoid getting married during the fall harvest. If you're in graduate school, avoid getting married during mid-term or end-of-semester exams. Are you an attorney with a case scheduled to go to trial in September? Don't get married in September!

Where Do You Want to Honeymoon?

Think about your honeymoon for a moment. If you plan to go to a Caribbean island, then getting married in September—during hurricane season—is not a great idea. Do you live in a hurricane zone? Or a fire zone? Think about the potential natural disasters that might interfere with either your wedding plans or your honeymoon destination.

If you plan to honeymoon in the Southern Hemisphere (South America, Australia, New Zealand, South Africa, the Maldives, etc.), remember that our summer is their winter. Think about whether you want to delay your honeymoon to accommodate conditions at your destination.

Avoid the End-of-Year Holidays

There are a lot of good reasons not to get married over major holidays like Thanksgiving and Christmas.

Travel is more expensive than usual at the holidays. If you never have to travel over the holidays, consider yourself lucky. Airports are a disaster. Flights are expensive. Hotels are expensive. Bad weather can snarl air traffic and the freeways. Asking friends and family to travel to your holiday wedding is asking a lot.

The holidays are hard on some people. For anyone who's lost a parent, sibling, or spouse, the holidays can be a sad time, not a joyous one. A lot of people like to hibernate over the holidays and avoid the fuss and the gatherings. These folks aren't going to want to come to your holiday wedding.

Also, your anniversary won't be as special if you get married at the holidays. Take it from someone who has multiple relatives with Christmas-adjacent birthdays: you want a day to yourself! Your wedding anniversary will always get lost in the hubbub around Christmas and New Year's Eve. It's way more fun to have your anniversary at a separate time of year.

Choose Two or Three Possible Dates

Once you've considered all of the above, try to come up with a couple of possible dates that will work for you. Having more than one potential date will make it much easier to find a venue. If you already have your heart set on a venue, then you'll have to work around their schedule. Many venues book a year (or more) in advance. But again, Fridays and Sundays are less popular days, and if your chosen venue can accommodate multiple weddings in a weekend, you'll have better luck if you can be flexible with your date.

Your Homework Assignment

Print a full-year calendar for your target wedding year. Pull out your personal and work calendars. Cross off all the dates that DON'T work for your wedding because of conflicts. Determine if there's a "best" time of year to travel to your preferred honeymoon destination. Home in on a particular season or month that works. Choose two or three potential wedding dates or an entire month that would work. Clear those with your VIPs—parents, siblings, best friends in the whole world—to make sure they don't have any conflicts. You now have your target dates. When you begin inquiring with venues, you can ask if they are available for any of those dates.

Choosing a location

I will delve deeply into how to conduct a venue search for your ceremony and reception in Chapter 4. For now, let's talk about the big picture. The world is a big place, and you have to narrow down where you want to get married to a particular city before you can start thinking about specific venues and reaching out to wedding professionals.

This might be super-easy for you. Maybe you've always known that you wanted to get married in your hometown (or some other, specific place) and your new fiancé(e) is totally on-board with that idea. Done and done. You can move on to the next section!

But for everyone else, keep reading.

Destination Weddings

Destination weddings, by definition, take place in a location where everyone, including the couple, has to travel. If you want to get married in a country other than the one where you live, then I strongly urge you to hire a local wedding planner in that destination. You will save so much time and money, not to mention headaches, if you hire a pro who is familiar with that destination and the local wedding pros.

Most destination weddings are on the smaller side, as far as guest count. Unless you're a celebrity or excessively wealthy (in which case you are almost certainly not reading this book), you're unlikely to ask 300 people to spend money travelling to an exotic location for your wedding. Destination wedding guest lists are usually under 50 people, and often more like 10–15 people.

If you're interested in getting married in a country where you are not a citizen, you'll need to do some serious research into the legalities. Acquiring a marriage license in a foreign country might involve things like blood tests, temporary visas, long-term stays, or extra paperwork. You'll also want to be sure that a marriage performed in a foreign country is legally valid in your home country.

One way to avoid this is to have a courthouse ceremony in your home country before you leave for your destination wedding. You'll have two wedding dates—your official, legal wedding date and your celebratory wedding date—but if you're okay with that, it will save you quite a bit of trouble. It's much easier to get a marriage license in the place where you live, and you won't have to worry about your destination wedding potentially not being legal.

Non-Destination Weddings

Even if you decide you don't want a true destination wedding, it can still be difficult to narrow down your options, especially if you and your fiancé(e) have moved away from your hometowns. Your most obvious options are: (1)

the place where you currently live, (2) your hometown, (3) your fiancé(e)'s hometown. It may go without saying, but the place where you currently live is the easiest option.

Planning a wedding requires visits to multiple venues to get a feel for them, meetings with potential wedding team members to interview them before hiring them, meetings with your actual wedding team after hiring them to discuss logistics, and then getting yourselves to the venue for the rehearsal and wedding. The closer you live to where the wedding will take place, the easier all of this will be.

If you live in a large, expensive city (New York, Boston, Washington DC, Chicago, Los Angeles, San Francisco, etc.), you'll have a million options, but they will be more expensive than options in smaller cities. Going just a short drive away from your large, expensive city can save you money while still being close enough to cut down on the hassle factor for you.

For example, I live and work in Sacramento, CA, which is only about 90 miles from San Francisco but has a much lower cost of living. Many of my clients live in San Francisco or the Bay Area but hold their weddings in Sacramento because it's less expensive. A lot of them are also originally from Sacramento, so their families live here, which is another factor to consider.

Depending on how large your families are, a significant percentage of your guest list could be made up of immediate and extended family members. Having your wedding in the city where there's a critical mass of family can make life easier for you and for them. It will cut down on their need to travel for the wedding, and you'll have a free place to stay when you come to town for all those venue visits and team meetings I mentioned above.

Another consideration when choosing your location is the availability of the type of venue you want for your wedding. If you've always dreamed of getting married among redwood trees, then you'll have to get married on the West Coast, regardless of where you live. If you really want a fashionable hotel ballroom wedding, then a big city is the place for you. I'll delve further into this in the next section when we talk about aesthetics.

Your Homework Assignment

Decide whether you want a destination wedding or not. Make a list of potential cities where it makes sense for you to get married. Cross off any that are too expensive or logistically difficult. Agree on the city where you will get married.

Now that you know how much you have available to spend on your wedding, a rough idea of how many guests you're inviting, what time of year you want to get married, and the city where you'll get married, it's time to focus on what your wedding will look and feel like. This is where those Pinterest boards really come in handy.

Choosing an overall aesthetic

Before you even get engaged, you are exposed to a lot of potentially useful information about weddings. Weddings are all around us: in real life, on TV and in the movies, in books and magazines, and in pop culture. Without even trying, you've been exposed to a whole lot of wedding ideas. Once you're engaged, spend a little time reflecting on some of the weddings you've seen or attended and figure out whether there are elements that you want or don't want to include in your wedding.

- Have you ever been to a wedding? Was there something in particular that you liked or disliked?
- Do you have siblings who have gotten married before you? Do you want your wedding to be similar to theirs, or the total opposite?
- Did your mom turn into a micro-manager when your sister got married and you really, really want to avoid that happening to you?
- Are you obsessed with watching *Say Yes to the Dress*, even though you've never put any serious thought into what you want your own wedding dress to look like?
- Did you get up ridiculously early to watch any (or all) of the royal weddings?
- Were you a bridesmaid for a friend who turned into a raving lunatic and you want to avoid that same fate?

Color scheme or palette

Wedding design, like any other design, needs a color palette to work within. Generally speaking, you want a three-color palette: two colors and a neutral. Your two colors can be complementary (opposite each other on a color wheel) or analogous (next to each other on a color wheel).

Complementary colors would be blue–orange, red–green, or yellow–purple. Analogous would be blue–green, red–orange, yellow–orange, green–purple, etc. Neutrals are black, white, grey, or metallics.

You can also think in terms of different hues or shades of a color. Pale pink and forest green with gold accents would be a complementary color scheme because pink is a type of red and forest green is a type of green, and red–green are opposite each other on the color wheel.

An easy place to start with your color palette is your favorite color, if you have one. Even a favorite flower can help you. If red roses are your absolute favorite, then a color palette including red is a great place to start.

The three-color palette is not set in stone. You can do a high-contrast wedding by choosing black/white/gold or choose one bold color and two neutrals, like red/gold/white, or even just one color and one neutral, like yellow/white. You could go all neutral with different shades of white: ivory/cream/beige and maybe a little metallic for some contrast.

Pinterest is a fantastic resource for discovering color palettes. Seeing them come to life might make you re-think something you don't think can work together. Just remember that if you keep seeing the same color palette over and over on Pinterest or Instagram, that means everyone is doing it. If you want your wedding to look unique, stay away from palettes that have been done to death.

Along those same lines, each year the Pantone Color Institute announces the Pantone Color of the Year. It takes a while for that particular color to filter down to weddings, so if you want to incorporate the Color of the Year for the year of your wedding, you'll be on the cutting edge, but it might be somewhat difficult to source items in that color.

Level of Formality

How formal do you want your wedding to be? Are you picturing guests in gowns and tuxedos, dancing the night away in a luxurious ballroom? Or sandals and bare feet on a beach somewhere? You need to decide on this early in the process, because it will determine what type of venue you search for. Ballgowns and tuxedos are out of place at the beach or on a ranch. Flip-flops and sundresses are inappropriate in a hotel ballroom or a botanical garden.

Time of day also plays into formality. There used to be some hard-and-fast rules about this: tuxedos would never be worn for a wedding that started before 6 pm, for example. But those rules have largely gone by the wayside. There are still a few guidelines though. If you're having a morning wedding (which is pretty uncommon, in and of itself), tuxedos are not appropriate because they are still generally thought of as evening attire. But if your ceremony is taking place in the late afternoon or evening, then most attire options are on the table.

You also need to take into account your guests when deciding on a level of formality for your wedding. Maybe you're picturing everyone in ballgowns and tuxedos, but are your friends and family the type of people who own tuxedos and ballgowns? It's inconvenient for your guests if you have a black-tie wedding and they all have to go rent tuxedos and gowns. If your guests are a mix of fancy-types and casual-types, you can go the "black-tie optional" route—those who have formal attire can wear it, while those who don't own formal attire can wear dressy attire they own or choose to rent formal attire.

Some Other Aesthetic Considerations

Have you ever seen the episode of *Friends* where Phoebe helps Joey decide which driving route to take from New York to Las Vegas by asking him a series of questions in rapid succession? This section is going to be a little like that! As I run through the following categories, answer as quickly as you can—just go with your gut. You can come back and think through the implications later.

- Dinner: buffet or plated?
- Music: band or DJ?
- Décor: colorful or monochromatic? Florals or greenery? Lush or sparse?
- Ceremony: religious or secular? In a church or not? Indoors or outdoors?
- Reception: indoors or outdoors?
- Ballroom or beach?
- Winery or ranch?
- Downtown or out in the country?
- Elegant dinner party or 10-keg rager?
- Timeless or trendy?

Answering these questions will help you later when you're looking for a venue and service providers to complete your wedding team. We'll discuss all of them in more detail in the next chapter.

Your Homework Assignment

Start a Pinterest board just for color schemes and spend a couple of days pinning to it. Then walk away for a day. Come back to it and figure out if there's a particular color scheme that dominates your board. Delete everything that doesn't fit in that color scheme.

Write down your answers to the questions above. Based on the trend, determine your overall level of formality, ranging from casual, to semi-formal, to black-tie optional, to black-tie.

Again on Pinterest, pin some wedding designs that appeal to you. Pin a lot of different things, as long as you like them. Put the board away for a few days, then come back to it and see which pins you like the best. Picture yourself at that wedding. This will help you narrow down your aesthetic choices. Delete pins that don't speak to you. I don't want you getting side-tracked or second-guessing yourself later.

Refer to your Pinterest board over the next few months as you begin to speak with wedding pros.

CHAPTER 4

Hiring Wedding Pros

In what order should you hire your wedding team?

There is a strategy to hiring your wedding team. In all but a few cases, you should start with your venue. The two instances where you won't begin with your venue are: 1) you already have your heart set on a particular professional (say, a photographer) and you want to work around their availability; or 2) you would like to hire a full-service wedding planner to help you with a venue search.

Generally speaking, you can't secure wedding pros until you have a wedding date, and you don't have a wedding date until you have a venue, which is why you should start with the venue. As I explained in the Design chapter, you'll want to be as flexible as possible with your target wedding date when you begin your venue search in order to have more options.

If you already know you want to hire a specific wedding pro and you know you're aiming for a fall wedding, your first email should be to that person or company to find out what their fall availability is. Feel free to explain that they are your top priority and that you want to choose your date based on their availability. If they can give you a few open dates to work with, it will make your venue search easier. They might be willing to put a "soft hold" on a couple of dates for you if you move quickly—they won't hold those dates for long, and they're under no obligation to do so.

Venue searches are time-consuming, so if you expect to hire a full-service wedding planner to help you with your venue search, be prepared to pay. Since you're reading this book, there's a good chance you're more of a "do-it-yourself" couple, in which case you probably aren't going to hire full-service planning help.

So here are three options for the order in which you should hire your wedding team.

Option 1: Traditional, i.e. secure the venue first

- Venue
- Wedding Coordinator
- Photographer and videographer
- Caterer
- DJ or band
- Wedding gown
- Bar services if not included with catering
- Florist
- Décor if separate from florist
- Stationer if you're having custom paper goods created
- Bakery
- Hair and makeup professionals
- Hotels and transportation
- Officiant
- Invitations ordered online
- Calligrapher
- Signage, guest book, favors, toasting flutes, cake cutting set (basically, anything you can order online from Etsy or similar sites)

Option 2: Category-specific

- Specific wedding service provider you want
- Venue
- Then proceed in the same order as above

Option 3: Full-Service help with venue search

- Wedding Planner
- Venue
- Then proceed in the same order as above

The reason I recommend hiring your wedding coordinator before your other wedding pros is that they will definitely have recommendations for you to consider. They can help you narrow down hundreds of wedding photographers to a handful of photographers, which you can then investigate more thoroughly.

Your Homework Assignment

Read the next three sections on Venue, Wedding Planner, and Wedding Coordinator. Discuss how much wedding planning help you need and can afford. If you decide to go the full-service planning route, start researching and interviewing planners right away. If you decide you can get by with only a coordinator, get started on your venue search.

Venue

Choosing your wedding venue can be one of the hardest, yet most important, things you have to do when wedding planning. You want to find a venue that's in your geographic target area, whether that's a state, region, or city. You have to find one that's available on your date and meets your aesthetic criteria. It has to fit within your budget. And it has to be reasonably convenient for your guests, or close to hotel accommodations.

Venue searches are time-consuming, and venues can book a year or more in advance, so don't put it off. As soon as you've finalized your budget, drafted a guest list, and defined your ideal time of year/date, location, and aesthetic, you need to start looking for a venue.

But where do you start?

How to Begin the Venue Search Process

Start with the most obvious options: have you attended any weddings in the area where you want to get married and did you like the venue? If so, start there. If not, become best friends with Google.

Search "wedding venue [insert geographic location]" and see what comes up. The first page of results will almost certainly be aggregator websites such as WeddingWire, The Knot, and Venue Vixens. These can be a good place for a broad overlook of a venue, but you really want to check out the venues' own websites. As a wedding pro with profiles on both WeddingWire and The Knot, I can tell you that my website has way more useful information on it than my profiles on those sites.

You can also try refining your search terms based on the aesthetic you're looking for, such as "garden wedding venue [your geographic location]" or "downtown loft wedding venue near me." Even without specifying your location or using the "near me," Google knows where you are and will show you results local to your location. This is helpful, unless you're looking for a venue somewhere other than where you live.

If you are searching for a venue outside of your physical geographic area, either use the city name in your search, or open a private browsing tab to conduct your search. This should prevent Google from defaulting to your current location.

Local wedding magazines can also be good resources for finding a venue, especially because you'll be able to see real weddings that took place there. Most reasonably large cities have some sort of local wedding guide or magazine. You can find them at grocery store or bookstore newsstands, or just Google "[insert your city or region] wedding magazine" and see what comes up.

And then there's always social media. Using hashtag searches can be a good way to find venues—try searching things like #sacramentoweddingvenue or #atlantaoutdoorwedding and see what comes up. If the poster geo-tagged the location with the venue name, then it will be obvious and you can Google-search the venue directly.

I will probably take some heat for saying this, but if you find a venue that doesn't have its own website, and only seems to have an online presence on aggregator websites, cross that venue off your list. If they aren't invested in their business enough to have a real website, they're not going to provide you with a quality experience. The same is true for all your major service categories. Nowadays it is both easy and inexpensive to have a website. Anyone who doesn't isn't taking their business seriously and won't take your wedding seriously either.

How to Keep Track of Your Venue Search

I know you don't want to hear this, but the answer is spreadsheets! (Hint: the answer is always spreadsheets. They are hands-down the best way to compile and track large amounts of data, especially where numbers are concerned.)

The main categories you want to track are: venue name, contact name, contact info, availability, capacity, cost, and what's included. Cost is a very tricky category, because venues vary wildly. Some include in-house catering and bar service, some include things like tables and chairs, some include nothing and you're paying just for the space. Use a column labeled "Notes" to keep track of any discrepancies in what each venue includes, or other useful information you discover during your survey.

If you truly want to be smart about your wedding budget, you must compare venues! There are so many wedding venues out there, and they all handle their pricing differently based on their own business needs. The only way to know that you're getting the best fit is to compare them. You don't have to compare a hundred different venues, but I strongly recommend you visit at least three. By comparing three venues, you can get a sense of the differences in approach that different venues take, but you won't overwhelm yourself with options.

What to Look for in a Wedding Venue

This book contains a venue questionnaire for you to use when interviewing or touring venues. There are a lot of questions to ask. Some of them will be answered by the website or as part of the venue site visit. But you will have to directly ask some of the more esoteric questions. You may also have specific questions of your own that apply only to your wedding, so be sure to jot those down before making any site visits.

The two most basic and important wedding venue requirements are whether they're available on your date and whether they can accommodate the number of guests you want to invite. That's why it's important to draft your guest list before you begin your venue search.

Some venues also have guest minimums, which can vary depending on whether it's a Saturday versus another day of the week, or an evening versus an afternoon. If you're planning a smaller guest list (under 100 people) find out if there are minimums.

What's included with the venue rental?

The next thing to look for is what's included. Refer back to your budget spreadsheet to make sure you don't get carried away by a beautiful venue before realizing you can't afford it. If your overall wedding budget is $50,000, and the venue has a $10,000 site fee that doesn't include catering, that venue is not a good fit for you.

Venues can be expensive. What are you getting for your money? Is it just the space, or are there other things included? Tables and chairs are the most common inclusions, but find out what the tables and chairs look like.

Most venues, if they include tables and chairs, are going to include the basics: a folding table that has to be covered with a tablecloth and white padded folding chairs. Those are totally fine if that's the look you want for your wedding.

But if you want nice wooden farm tables with wooden cross-back chairs, you'll have a harder time finding a venue that includes those. If that's the route you want to go, then a venue that doesn't include tables and chairs (and therefore doesn't charge as much to rent their space) might be a good option for you.

It's also important to note how many tables and chairs are included. If the venue includes tables and chairs for 150 guests, but you're inviting 200 guests, you'll have to rent tables and chairs to make up the difference. Factor that into your venue comparisons.

How nice are the restrooms?

Are the restrooms inside or outside? How elegant are they? Do you need to bring in your own restrooms? Does the venue provide restroom amenity baskets or do you need to supply them? (Think mouthwash strips, hand cream, mints, feminine products, hairspray, tissues.)

Is there space for the couple to get ready?

This is especially important if the venue is out in the country and not close to any hotels. Where is the couple going to get ready? If you are two brides or two grooms, is one of you going to end up in a space that's clearly meant for the other gender? I've never once seen a venue with gender-neutral getting ready spaces. It's always a "bridal suite" and a "groom's suite." One is always light and bright, and the other is always dark and masculine. (If you are a same-sex couple and you rule out a venue because of its overly gendered getting ready spaces, you should definitely tell the venue. The only way they will change is if it costs them business.)

Is there enough space for your bridesmaids or groomsmen to be with you? Is there ample room and natural light for your hair and makeup team (and for your photographer)?

Is there an additional fee for the getting ready space? Or a cleaning fee?

What do the grounds look like?

Think about your photo ops. Are you doing a first-look photo session? What about wedding party photos? Family photos? Does the venue or property have the type of scenery you want for those photos?

Inquire about sunset—which way is west, and what are the sunsets like there? Use location tagging on Instagram to help you out here. Search for your venue and see what photos have been posted. I personally tag the venue in all of the real wedding photos I post to my social media to help others with this type of research.

How late can your wedding go?

Noise ordinances vary by city or county. If you want to party into the wee hours of the morning, this is going to be an important question to ask at your venue visit. Most venues will have a contracted end time of 10 pm or 11 pm. Some will allow you to go later for an extra fee, but for some it's a hard cut-off with no room for negotiation.

In the same vein, how long is the rental period and when do you get access to the space? Some venues give you access all day, some all weekend, and some have specific times. For example, maybe you don't get access until noon, but you're having a 3 pm ceremony. You're probably going to need to do hair and makeup off-site and then maybe just get into your wedding gown at the venue.

You'll also want to find out when they usually hold rehearsals. If you're getting married on a Sunday, you're likely not going to be able to hold your rehearsal Saturday afternoon because another wedding will be going on. You might have to hold your rehearsal Saturday morning, or even Thursday afternoon.

If you're getting married at a winery, you may have to work around their tasting room hours or special events.

If many of your family members and wedding party members will be coming in from out of town for your wedding rehearsal, you'll want it to be as close as possible to your wedding day to ensure that they can all attend.

Is catering done in-house or not?

If your venue does catering in-house, that means you will not be able to bring in your own caterer. So you need to make sure that their food meets your expectations, if food is important to you. Keep in mind that you probably won't be able to schedule a tasting until after you've booked your wedding there, so you'll have to rely on other people's opinions.

Check their online reviews to see what people are saying about the food. Ask your wedding planner if she is familiar with the venue and their food. (Generally speaking, the planner, DJ, and photographer are always fed at weddings, so while they may not be getting the exact same meal as the guests, they probably have an opinion about the venue or caterer's food.)

Do you know anyone else who has gotten married at this venue, even if it's a friend-of-a-friend? Ask them what they thought. Put out a call on social media. Do what you have to!

If you already have someone in mind for other services, it's also important to find out whether you must use a venue's preferred list or if you can bring in your own team members. Most venues are fine with you going off the list for planners, florists, and photographers. They get more particular when it comes to DJs (because of electricity requirements) and caterers (because of insurance requirements).

You also should find out whether or not you can bring in your own alcohol. Some venues will let you do this, no problem. Some will let you do it, but they'll charge you a per-bottle fee (called a "corkage fee"). And some won't let you do it at all. Buying your own alcohol can be a huge money-saver for you, so this is an important question to ask.

Your Homework Assignment

If you're going to do your own venue search, start by following the guidelines above. Find a few venues you're interested in and start researching them online, filling in the venue spreadsheet as you go. Start by emailing venues to check availability on your potential dates. Schedule site visits for your top three that meet your initial criteria: available, within your budget, fit your overall aesthetic.

Use the Venue Questionnaire to help you ask the right questions. Find the Venue Questionnaire at www.risajamesevents.com/wedding-questionnaires. If you need to rent a lot of décor items or a tent, find the Rental/Tent Questionnaire at the same link.

Full-Service Wedding Planners & Designers

Planning a wedding is hard. You've probably never done this before, and you don't know what you don't know. Rather than making mistakes and potentially forgetting something major, it might make sense for you to bring in a professional.

Reasons to Consider Hiring a Full-Service Planner

A Wedding Planner Saves You Time

You would be amazed at the number of hours that go into planning a wedding. The number of emails. The number of phone calls. There are a million and one details, and a team of wedding pros to communicate with. Having a wedding planner be the point person for all of that can save you loads of time and headaches.

Finding Wedding Pros

Do you know all the best wedding pros in the city where you're getting married? Probably not. But a wedding planner does. They know their work, their styles, and their personalities. A planner can save you the trouble of meeting with the wrong people by connecting you with the right service providers off the bat.

Scheduling Meetings

It takes a surprising amount of back-and-forth communication to set up meetings and discuss wedding-related items. You have a job. You can't always be available for a call with one of your wedding pros, and your boss would appreciate it if you focused on your job during working hours, instead of planning your wedding. It is literally your wedding planner's job to handle scheduling meetings and playing phone tag and doing those things that you shouldn't be doing while you're supposed to be working.

Doing Research

While it can be fun to browse Pinterest and pin lots of ideas to your wedding board, when you need a specific item or you need to know the answer to a specific question, Pinterest is not your best bet. Your wedding planner can track down the perfect wedding favor, or figure out how many bottles of wine and beer you need, or find the best place to create your online honeymoon registry.

Tracking Details

To have a wedding, you first need to create a budget. Then you need to track all your expenses to be sure you're staying within budget. You need a guest list, and then you have to track all the responses and maybe even what everyone is having for dinner. You need a wedding website where you can post all the relevant information about your wedding so you're not fielding 101 emails from friends and family with questions about the best hotel to stay in, or what there is to do in the city where you're getting married. Your wedding planner can help you with ALL of those things!

Designing Your Wedding

Maybe you're not in love with Pinterest. Maybe you don't have a million ideas about what you want your wedding to look like. Your wedding planner will have tons of ideas. And even if you do have lots of ideas of your own, a planner can help you narrow them down into a coherent design scheme. Wedding planners live and breathe weddings. They know what's been done to death and what's on the cutting edge. Let a planner put their knowledge to work for you.

A Wedding Planner Saves You Money

Yes, you have to spend money to hire a wedding planner, but they can save you money too. Some wedding planners have access to special discounts that couples working without a planner do not. And some wedding pros (like DJs and photographers) will give you a discount if you're working with a planner because they know their job will be so much easier with a planner handling the details.

Some planners have special relationships with pros they work with often, which results in special pricing for you that you wouldn't be able to get otherwise.

Furthermore, you won't make costly mistakes or overspend on something if you have a wedding planner guiding you through the process.

A Wedding Planner Saves You Stress

This point cannot be overstated! Having a professional by your side goes a long way toward easing your mind. There's so much to keep track of and so many things to do. If you have a wedding planner, the burden is lifted from you, and you can actually have fun with the planning process.

When to Hire a Wedding Planner

You can hire a wedding planner either before or after you've secured a wedding venue. Many planners will help you conduct a venue search, but those are time-consuming, so expect to pay extra for that service.

If you wait until after securing a venue to hire a planner, it's best to do so before hiring the rest of your wedding team. One of a wedding planner's most valuable services is helping you put together the ideal wedding team. You short-change yourself by hiring too many other pros before hiring your planner.

What is a Wedding Designer?

There is a category of wedding professional called a "wedding designer." They don't do any planning for you, but they will design and execute an overall décor theme for your wedding.

Generally, they'll put together a proposal including two or three different design themes, with lots of photos to illustrate their ideas. Areas they'll cover include florals, color scheme, accent pieces (lounge furniture or other décor items), table settings (plates, chargers, linens, flatware, glasses), invitation suites and other stationery items (menus, programs, place cards, escort cards, table numbers, thank you notes), and possibly even a cake design.

Once you choose the design that you like, the designer will execute it for you. They'll hire the rental company to provide all the pieces included in their proposal. They'll engage the florist and work with her to design all the floral elements of the wedding (arch décor, table centerpieces, accent arrangements, personal flowers like bouquets and boutonnières). They'll order all your stationery items, working with you along the way.

Then on your wedding day, they (and their team) are at your wedding to set up all the décor and make it look beautiful for you. You will still need a planner or coordinator to handle the logistics of your day. More on that below.

Wedding Planner Approach

Some wedding planners offer full design services, and some don't. Again, if full design is something you're interested in, just ask the planners you speak with whether (and how) they handle design.

There's another important distinction between planners that we should cover before we get into the details of what a planner does: whether or not they have a dedicated implementation team with whom they always work.

Planners with a Dedicated Implementation Team

Some planners, usually the ones who work on high-end luxury weddings (those with six- and seven-figure budgets), have a team of wedding pros that they ALWAYS work with because they know they can trust them. Those pros usually include floral designers, caterers, bakeries, rental companies, lighting companies, and décor companies. Bands and DJs may also be included. Generally, photo/video and hair/makeup are not part of the team, and you would hire those professionals separately.

When you hire one of these planners, you are contracting with and paying the planner, and they are contracting with and paying the rest of the team members. You will have very little direct contact with those subcontractors (which sounds so construction-y, but that's basically what they are), and your planner will always be with you if you do meet with them.

In this case, the planner usually charges a mark-up on all contracted services. (And a reputable planner will be upfront with you about this). For example, if the lighting company would normally charge $5000 for your lighting package, you might instead be paying $5500 because the planner charges a 10% fee for managing the lighting company.

Keep in mind though that the lighting company is probably also offering the planner a discounted rate, because they know each other and have worked together before and have a good relationship. So if you were to hire the lighting company on your own for the same package, your price could be $6000. So even with the planner's markup, you could still save money. (It's all complicated and rather opaque, unfortunately.)

Planners Who Work with a Variety of Service Providers

It's more common for wedding planners to work with a variety of service providers, depending on the specific event and the needs of the client. All planners have their favorite, go-to pros in different categories, but most of us also enjoy working with new (to us) pros and getting to know other people in the industry.

If you already know a photographer or DJ that you want to work with on your wedding, most planners will gladly welcome them to the team. One caveat: if you want your college roommate who used to DJ frat parties to DJ your wedding, many professional planners will balk at this. DJing and emceeing a wedding is a professional skill. Professional planners like to work with other professionals because it makes the entire event run more smoothly.

What Does a Wedding Planner Do?

Now that we've covered some of the different types of wedding planners, let's talk about what they actually do, generally speaking. Everyone runs their business somewhat differently, but for the most part, this is what you can expect a full-service planner to handle. We'll discuss wedding coordination in the next section.

Puts Together Your Wedding Team

A wedding planner helps you put together the best wedding team. Think of your wedding planner as a matchmaker. Taking into account your personality, your overall wedding vibe, and your budget, the planner will reach out to the pros they think are most likely to benefit your wedding day.

They'll handle the initial communication to the service provider to see if they're available on your date, and then they'll facilitate a meeting or a phone call for the three of you to discuss your wedding and your needs.

You'll sign a contract with individual service providers and be responsible for payments to them directly, but your planner will facilitate the contracting process.

Manages Communication

In addition to the initial hiring phase, your planner will also manage communication among your wedding team throughout the planning process. A flurry of communication is common at the beginning of the process, and then much more as the wedding date approaches and logistical details are being worked out.

Most weddings have between 8 and 12 team members, so communicating with all of them and keeping everyone on the same page takes a lot of time. Having a planner as your point person takes this responsibility off of you.

Handles Menu and Rental Items

Your wedding planner will work with you and your caterer to put together a menu for your wedding, and will manage your rental order as well. Some caterers provide no tabletop items (plates, flatware, glasses, linens). Some provide only basic white or black linens with basic china and glassware.

Some caterers work regularly with a rental company and can manage your rental order. But if you want to rent décor items as well as specialty linens and tabletop items, it's best to have your planner manage the entire order.

Orders Stationery Products

Most full-service wedding planners will help you order your invitation suite and all the other stationery items you need for your wedding: menu cards, programs, signage, table numbers, escort cards, seating charts, etc. They often have discounts that they share with clients to get the best pricing.

If you want a fully custom stationery suite, your planner can connect you with a stationery designer who can create whatever your heart desires. They can also connect you with calligraphers to custom-create your signage and address your wedding invitations.

Keeps You on Track

A good wedding planner will keep tabs on all of your contracts, deadlines, payment dates, and budget to make sure nothing falls through the cracks. Most service providers require an initial deposit to guarantee your date, but the final payment dates can range from one month before the wedding to the day of the wedding. Your planner will make sure you don't miss any payments.

Having an overall budget broken down into individual categories will ensure that you don't spend more money than you anticipated. Your planner can track all your expenses and enter them into a budget template to keep you on track.

Attends Meetings with You

Your planner will attend all your meetings to facilitate the conversation and make sure all the details are covered. For example, when you meet with your florist to discuss design, your planner will be with you to make sure you order the right number of centerpieces and accent pieces, and can provide information on which rental items and linen colors are being ordered.

Your DJ planning meetings are also an important component to making sure your wedding day flows smoothly. Having your planner there with you helps ensure that everyone is on the same page.

Your planner will also visit the venue with you multiple times. Any planning meetings you have with your venue, your planner will be there too.

Manages Guest Logistics

Wedding planners also make necessary arrangements to help your out-of-town guests have a smooth travel experience. They can arrange hotel room blocks for guests and line up group transportation, such as shuttles or buses, depending on how many guests need transportation. They can also help you put together hotel welcome bags for your guests when they check into their hotels.

Creates Floor Plans and Seating Charts

As your wedding date gets closer, your planner will put together a floor plan so you know where the tables will be located, where the cake will be, where the buffet tables will be, where the dance floor will be, etc. They can also help you with your seating chart, which is the worst part of planning a wedding!

Only you can decide who will sit where, because you know the interpersonal dynamics of your friends and family. But many wedding planners have online tools that can make the process a little easier for you.

Provides Advice and Guidance

A wedding planner also serves as a counselor for you throughout the planning process. If you have questions or need advice or need help finding something particular, your planner can help. They have loads of knowledge and experience that they bring to your wedding.

Ultimately, when you hire a planner, you're not just hiring them for the tasks that they perform, but you're also hiring them for their knowledge and expertise. You're only going to plan one wedding, but they've planned dozens and dozens. Let them help you!

Overlap Between a Wedding Planner and a Wedding Coordinator

Once your wedding day is only a month or two away, much of what a wedding planner does overlaps with what a wedding coordinator does. The next section dives deep into a wedding coordinator's responsibilities, and how they differ from a full-service planner or designer.

Your Homework Assignment

Read the next section on wedding coordinators, then decide whether a full-service planner or a coordinator is right for you.

Wedding Coordinator

Wedding Planner & Wedding Coordinator Overlap

The vast majority of items a wedding coordinator handles will also be handled by a full-service wedding planner. Everyone runs their business slightly differently, but for the most part, these are standard services that a wedding coordinator will provide, regardless of whether you've hired them for full-service planning or coordination only.

As outlined in the previous section, a wedding planner provides much more than a coordinator in the way of actual services, but in both cases, you're getting a wealth of knowledge and experience that they will put to good use for your wedding. Hiring a planner or coordinator will always be money well-spent. (And I'm not just saying that because this is how I make my living. You won't realize how much you need a planner or coordinator until it's too late.)

Don't Call it a Day-of Coordinator

I'm going to climb on my high horse for a moment and explain why a wedding coordinator is not a "day-of coordinator." In a nutshell, there's no such thing as a day-of coordinator. This is an unhelpful misnomer that has somehow been perpetuated by the wedding industry. No one can show up on your wedding day and make it run smoothly without a lot of background work.

Weddings are extraordinarily complex affairs with multiple service providers and a ton of moving pieces. Everything must be carefully calculated in order to run smoothly. The more information your coordinator has beforehand, the better your wedding will go.

Most coordinators will start working with a couple 4 to 12 weeks before their wedding and will almost always meet with the couple at least once before the wedding weekend. For this reason alone, calling it "day-of" is a vast understatement.

Creating Your Wedding Day Timeline

One of the most valuable services a wedding coordinator provides is creating your wedding day timeline, or schedule. This is the blueprint for your wedding day. Without it, nothing will happen on time, and some things might not happen at all.

Perhaps you're thinking, "Well, my DJ (or photographer) offers a day-of timeline as part of their package, so I don't need a coordinator." No disrespect to all the photographers and DJs out there, but their timeline isn't going to be as thorough as your wedding planner/coordinator's timeline.

Think of it this way: your photographer's job is to capture amazing photos of your day. Your DJ's job is to play awesome music that's going to keep your guests dancing all night long. It's NOT their job to create a timeline for you, even if they include that in their package. The reason they include that in their package is that they've learned over the years that not all couples are smart enough to hire a planner or coordinator, and that without a timeline, the day will be a disaster. So they step in to fill that gap.

But you know what? Your photographer and DJ will LOVE you if you hire a planner or coordinator. Why? Because it makes their job easier and it allows them to focus on what you really hired them to do.

When your planner or coordinator prepares your wedding timeline, they aren't focusing only on the photos that need to be taken or the special moments that require special songs. Yes, they focus on those things too, but they focus on so much more.

The timeline actually begins before your wedding day, with any deliveries that are happening the day before and with your rehearsal. Your photographer and DJ don't really care what happens the day before your wedding.

On your wedding day, the timeline begins with your full hair and makeup schedule, which can be elaborate if you have a lot of bridesmaids having professional services. All of the arrival times or drop-off times will be included. Special situations will be considered. For example, if your florist is going to be placing fresh flowers on your cake, someone needs to make sure the cake is delivered while the florist is still on-site setting up. Only your planner or coordinator is going to bring that level of detail to your timeline.

Your planner or coordinator will also have a full description of what happens during the ceremony. Not only which songs will play, but the order in which people will walk down the aisle, who will be paired with whom, who will be sitting in the first row (and in which seats), how the hand-off of the bride will go, who's the last person to walk down the aisle before the song changes from wedding party to bride. Lots of details! The planner/coordinator will also be with you and your wedding party to cue you when it's time to walk down the aisle.

Planner timelines also include all the things that your photographer and DJ care about: when is the first-look, what time is the first dance, are there parent dances, will there be a bouquet toss, is the cake being cut before dinner or after? But they also put in things like what time the salad course is served, when the meal for your wedding team will be available, and when coffee and dessert will be served.

Another valuable timeline-related service that only your planner or coordinator will provide is making sure the entire wedding team is on the same page, literally. They talk to your other wedding team members in the weeks leading up to your wedding to find out those arrival times and to make sure the cake and the florist will be there at the same time. They ask your photographer how long they need for the first-look or for family portraits because every photographer has their own style and workflow.

They share the final timeline with your venue, caterer, photographer, DJ, florist, rental company, bakery, transportation company, tent company — everyone who needs to know what's happening and when. That way everyone knows the plan, and there are no surprises on your wedding day!

I like to think of a wedding coordinator as the conductor of an orchestra. The orchestra is made up of lots of individual musicians who all have their part to play. But if they all just do their own thing, you end up with chaos. They need the conductor to help them keep tempo and to know when their section should begin playing and when their section should stop playing. An orchestra without a conductor is just noise. An orchestra with a conductor is music.

It's the same for your wedding. A wedding without a coordinator is chaos. A wedding with a coordinator is magic.

Managing Your Rehearsal

You also need a wedding planner or coordinator to manage your wedding rehearsal. This is especially important if your officiant is a friend or family member rather than a professional clergy person or wedding officiant.

Wedding ceremonies are highly choreographed. Someone needs to be in charge of telling everyone what to do, where to stand, and when to come in. That's what your wedding coordinator does. The rehearsal is literally a practice run of your ceremony so that on your big day, when all the guests are there and the photographer is snapping away, people don't look lost and confused. Again, coordinators bring order to chaos.

Handling Set-up on Your Wedding Day

Setting up for a wedding is a multi-hour process. Your wedding team members pretty much handle their own set-up, but they always have questions. Do you want them to be texting or calling you repeatedly while you're trying to relax and get ready? Or would you rather have a designated point person for them to go to? Your planner or coordinator is that point person. They will be there during set-up to answer questions and make decisions on your behalf so no one has to bug you, and you get to enjoy yourself on your wedding day.

You also probably have a lot of your own items to set up. Things like your guest book, signage, seating chart or escort cards, table numbers, programs, assigned ceremony seat tags, menu cards, favors—all the items you put a lot of work into designing and ordering. Who do you think is going to set that up? Not your venue, caterer, or florist. They have their own things to worry about. You and your family? Nope. You've got better things to do. That's what your coordinator is for!

Why Your Mom Can't Coordinate Your Wedding

You might be thinking that your mom, or your auntie, or your really organized cousin or friend can handle all that set-up for you. Sure they can. But they won't get to actually have any fun at your wedding. No one can both coordinate and be a guest at a wedding. There are too many things to do.

Your mom and your friends and family should have fun at your wedding. They should have a leisurely morning getting ready and hanging out with you, and they should be free to socialize and chat with friends during the event. They won't get to do any of that if you ask them to set up all your stuff and coordinate your wedding.

Not to mention the fact that unless your mom is a wedding professional, she's not going to have the knowledge or experience to make your wedding day the best it can be. When you hire a planner or coordinator, you're not just hiring them for the services they perform. You're also hiring them for their experience, their expertise, and their knowledge.

Keeping Things on Schedule

Your wedding day will fly by. You will blink, and it will be over. There is so much happening, and so many people to talk to, and so much dancing to be done. If you expect all those special moments to happen (and happen on time), you need someone to be watching the clock and watching the schedule.

Your wedding planner or coordinator will be the person watching the clock. They aren't there to have fun—they are there to work. They are there to make sure you and your family and friends have fun.

What is a venue coordinator?

When you start researching wedding venues, some of them might say that they include a coordinator. This is very different than hiring your own wedding coordinator.

There are two types of venue coordinators. One type is really just there to watch over the venue, answer venue-specific questions, and make sure you don't burn the place down. This type of coordinator is going to do almost nothing to help you with your actual wedding.

The other type of venue coordinator is advertised as more of a "day-of coordinator" to help you with your wedding. They might prepare a timeline for you. They'll coordinate your ceremony by lining up your wedding party and telling everyone when to walk in. And they'll be on hand throughout the evening to keep your wedding running reasonably smoothly.

But there are important differences between a venue coordinator and an independent wedding coordinator.

The venue coordinator works for the venue, not for you

This sounds obvious, but think about it for a moment. The venue coordinator is employed by the venue. The venue pays them a salary. They owe their loyalty to the venue, not to the clients.

If a situation arises that results in tension between you and the venue, they are going to side with the venue every time and work to resolve the matter in a way that is most favorable to the venue. And you can't fault them for that—it's their job.

When you hire an independent wedding coordinator, they work for you. Most wedding coordinators are self-employed, so their loyalties can be with their clients. They are always going to do the best that they can to maximize every opportunity for their clients. Sure, they don't want to jeopardize their relationship with a venue, but you're the one paying their fee, so you are their priority.

The venue coordinator is overworked

Most wedding venues handle anywhere from 50 to 300 weddings per year. Depending on how many coordinators they have on staff, the one assigned to you could be responsible for 100 weddings per year. That's a lot of weddings.

Chances are also good that your venue and your coordinator have more than one wedding in any given weekend—possibly even more than one wedding on any given day, depending on how large the facility is. They are pulled in many different directions.

When you hire an independent wedding coordinator, their focus is on you and your wedding alone. Some wedding planners/coordinators, like me, work essentially alone. I only book one wedding per weekend so I can give my clients my full attention.

Some planners/coordinators have associate planners on their staff. In this case, the company can take on more than one wedding in a given day or weekend, but each wedding still has a dedicated coordinator or planner whose sole focus is that wedding.

Either way, when you hire an independent wedding coordinator, you get someone who is more focused on you than a venue coordinator can possibly be.

The venue coordinator can't give you the personal attention you deserve

This ties into the above, but venue coordinators can't be with you every step of the way like an independent coordinator can be. They just don't have the time to answer all your questions and reply to all your emails.

They also may not be able to set up all the personal touches you want to add to your wedding. Even though you're hiring a team of pros, you will still probably have things like a guest book, escort cards, seating chart, table numbers, favors, etc. Someone needs to set up all those items.

Your venue coordinator may or may not handle something like that. Your independent wedding coordinator will definitely be able to handle that for you.

Venue coordinators work hard, and they add value to your wedding. But they aren't a substitute for a wedding coordinator that you hire separately. Your wedding coordinator and the venue coordinator will work together as a team to make sure your day is as awesome as it should be, so don't fall into the trap of thinking that you don't need both.

Your Homework Assignment

Decide whether you need and can afford a full-service planner. If so, start researching and interviewing them right away. If not, circle back to the Venue section and begin your venue search. You can research and interview wedding coordinators after you've secured a venue and have a specific wedding date on the books. But don't wait too long, because most coordinators also offer full-service planning, and their calendars can fill up 6 to 12 months in advance.

Use the Coordinator Questionnaire to help you ask the right questions. Find the Coordinator Questionnaire at www.risajamesevents.com/wedding-questionnaires.

Photographer

How To Search for a Wedding Photographer

You are going to put a lot of time, effort, and money into your wedding. When it's all over, you will have only two things: your memories and your photos. Hiring the right photographer is a super-important part of wedding planning. Luckily, it's easier than ever to research wedding photographers!

Instagram is your best friend when it comes to looking for a wedding photographer. It's like having access to everyone's portfolio all at once. Just search #weddingphotography or #weddingphotographer to get started. (But I warn you, there are millions of posts with those hashtags, so you'll need to refine it in order to make any substantial progress with your search.)

If you want to geographically refine your search, add your city name or region to the hashtag. For example #pnwweddingphotographer or #miamiweddingphotographer. You will find a bounty of posts.

After you've glanced through a few portfolios, you will start to get a sense of the different styles of shooting and editing. Some photographers use a photojournalism style of photography. They are there to capture the story of the day as it unfolds. They are masters of seeing those candid moments that might be missed in the hustle and bustle. When you look at your photos after the wedding, you'll be grateful they were there to capture those moments.

Other photographers have a more classical portrait style. These photographers often have lighting setups that they bring with them (sometimes rather elaborate setups). If you look at enough wedding photos, you'll start to be able to recognize the difference between the portrait photographers and the photojournalists. One style will probably resonate more with you than another, so pay attention to how the photos make you feel.

Most photographers will also talk about their style and philosophy in the About Me section of their website, so if you find a photographer on Instagram that you like, be sure to stalk their website a little bit to see even more of their work. Many photographers also have visual blogs where they'll post 20-50 images from the same wedding. This gives you a great sense of how they shoot over the course of the day, and not just the one or two photos they post to their IG account.

Another area where photographers really vary is in their editing style. If you spend enough time on Instagram, you may have noticed a trend over the past few years toward very light, bright, airy images. Maybe you love that style, or maybe you prefer more vivid, high-contrast photos with rich colors and the interplay between shadows and light. Again, pay attention to which photos capture your eye the most.

While most photographers could vary their editing style to fit your request, many of them will not. They've spent years developing their style and their brand. They want people to recognize that style as theirs, so they are usually unwilling to alter it. If you like a particular photographer's style, you should try to hire that photographer and not try to get some other photographer to imitate their style.

Don't forget about your budget! Photography should account for about 10 percent of your overall budget (and that includes videography, if you're doing that as well). Some photographers put package and pricing information on their websites; some don't. If you find a photographer you like who is out of your price range, you have two options: 1) Find another photographer you like whose prices are lower, or 2) find another budget category that you can cut in order to allocate those funds to your photography line item.

When you inquire with a photographer, be honest about your budget. There are a lot of talented photographers out there. I assure you that you can find one whose style you like and whose services you can afford.

If you're interested in having a photo booth at your wedding, you can inquire with potential photographers and DJs to see if they offer that service. Otherwise, there are specialty photo booth companies that you can hire.

How Many Hours of Wedding Photography Do You Need?

As part of your photographer search, you'll see a wide variety of packages offered by different photographers. Some include only six hours; some go up to 12 hours. But how do you figure out how much photography coverage you need?

The answer is always, "more than you think." Most weddings last around five to six hours from the start of the ceremony to the end of dancing. So you might think a wedding photography package that includes six hours of coverage would be sufficient, right? Wrong.

The wedding day begins well before the ceremony starts. Hair and makeup will begin at least a few hours before the ceremony, and perhaps quite early in the morning if you have a lot of bridesmaids who are all having hair and makeup done. The "getting ready" time with your attendants and mom is a chance to drink a little Champagne, catch up on everyone's life, and relax a bit before the big show begins. It can be really fun to have photos of this time.

And no wedding album is complete without some shots of a bride finalizing her dress, veil, and jewelry, or a groom putting on his tie and cufflinks. But if you haven't budgeted enough time for the photographer to capture these memories, all you'll have is some poorly lit and badly framed iPhone photos. And nobody wants that.

The "getting ready" portion of the day is also when your photographer snaps photos of the dress hanging in the window, shoes and jewelry staged for display, and the full invitation suite. These are classic photos that you don't want to miss out on.

Extra photographer time becomes even more important if you're having a first-look photo session. If you are, all the wedding party photos and the immediate family group photos will also probably be scheduled to happen pre-ceremony. This all can take 60–90 minutes.

On the back end, you can usually get away with letting the photographers leave before the end of the reception, unless you're planning a grand exit, in which case you'll want the photographers on hand to capture that. But with no grand exit, your coordinator can usually structure your timeline so that the major events (first dance, parent dances, cake cutting, bouquet/garter toss) are done well before the end of the reception.

You only need so many photos of guests dancing. You want to make sure the photographer is present for at least some of the dancing, to capture the mood of the party. But usually the last hour of the reception is just more of the same, from a photography standpoint.

So back to the original question: how many hours of wedding photography do you need? I recommend at least eight. Here's an abbreviated sample timeline:

12–2:30 getting ready
3–4:30 first-look/wedding party/family photos
5–5:30 ceremony
5:30–6:30 cocktail hour
6:30–7:45 grand entrance, dinner, toasts
7:45–8 special dances
8–8:30 dancing
8:30–8:45 cake cutting and bouquet/garter toss
8:45–10 or 11 dancing

If you book your photographer for eight hours, she can arrive around 1 pm to capture the getting ready time, and depart around 9 pm, once all the scheduled events have happened. Anything less, and you're going to find that you have to skimp on getting photos of everything.

When you find a photographer you like, if their packages don't fit your needs exactly, don't be afraid to reach out anyway. There's a good chance that they can customize something just for you.

Will the additional hours of coverage cost you more? Yes. Will it be worth it? Yes. When you look at photos from your wedding five, ten, fifty years after the day, will you remember the extra money you spent on a photographer? Absolutely not.

Do You Need a Second Wedding Photographer?

A lot of couples simply don't know whether they'll want or need a second photographer at their wedding. Most wedding photographers can capture everything as a solo shooter. But there are a few cases where a couple might want to consider choosing a photography package that includes a second photographer. If any of the following scenarios apply to you, you'll want a second photographer.

1. You're getting ready in two different places, and you want photos of both of you getting ready. As discussed above, photographers usually put together a "getting ready" gallery, and with two photographers, you get to see what your partner was doing during this time. If you're getting ready in separate areas of the same property, it's not difficult for one photographer to hop over from one group to the other to get a few photos of putting on the dress, shoes, veil, ties, boutonnières, etc. But if you are getting ready in two different places, you will need a second photographer to be at the second location.

2. You want photos of the details at the reception, but your ceremony is being held in a different location. If the ceremony and reception are in the same location, the photographer can usually take 20 minutes to photograph the reception space before the ceremony begins. But if your ceremony and reception are in different locations, you will miss out on photos of all those details if you only have one photographer. The photographer won't be able to get to the reception and take detail photos before the guests get there.

3. You're having a ceremony in a church. Two photographers will sometimes be better for big church weddings because some churches frown on having a photographer moving all over the place during the ceremony and worship service. If you are getting married in a church, check with them to find out if they have restrictions on photography.

4. You want the most photos possible. With two photographers, one person can be "behind the scenes" before you walk down the aisle, while the other photographer is stationed near the altar to capture the close-ups. You get two different perspectives. You'll also have multiple

shots and angles of the rest of the wedding, which gives you more options when putting together your wedding album.

5. You need to take photos after the ceremony. If you're taking family photos after the ceremony, the second photographer can go on to cocktail hour to get candid photos of guests while you finish photos with family. This is especially useful if you're not doing a first-look photo session. With the photographer tied up doing couple, wedding party, and family shots during the entire cocktail hour, they will not have an opportunity to capture any photos of guests during that time.

6. You're expecting more than 150 guests. Photographers always do their best to capture as many guests as they can, but if you're planning a large guest list, it's helpful to have a second person there to cover more ground.

My personal recommendation is to have a second shooter. You will get more photos, and there's less of a chance that something will be missed.

Should You Have a First-Look Photo Session?

Something that's become very popular in recent years is a "first-look" photo session. Traditionally, a couple only saw each other for the first time on their wedding day when the bride walked down the aisle. But that can be a little stressful, especially if you are shy or private, because all eyes are on you at this special moment.

A first-look is a great way to preserve the special moment when you see your spouse-to-be for the first time on your wedding day, but keep it more private. It's typically just the couple and one or two photographers at a bit of a distance to capture the moment but to give the couple space. Some couples choose to have their parents or wedding party nearby so they can also witness the moment.

You have options when it comes to staging your first-look photos. Often, the photographer will position one partner with their back to the other. The other partner approaches from a distance, taps them on the shoulder, they turn, and then they see each other for the first time. Or the partners are positioned back-to-back and they turn around at the same time.

If the couple is getting ready inside a historical home or other pretty indoor space, the photographer can place one partner inside a room and have the other one enter. Some couples opt to get ready together, so there's no real "first-look," but all the getting ready photos have them together, which is fun.

A first-look session is especially helpful if either one of you is especially prone to tearing up or crying when you get emotional. This gives you a chance to get the emotion settled early in the day so that when you walk down the aisle, you can focus on the joy of the moment, instead of worrying about tears ruining your makeup.

Another big advantage to having a first-look is that once the couple photos are finished, you can do all (or most) of the family and wedding party photos. Finishing those before the ceremony lets you actually enjoy your cocktail hour and have fun with your guests. Couples who opt not to do a first-look generally miss their entire cocktail hour because they are busy with photos. If you do a first-look session, I recommend trying to fit in a sunset photo session as well, usually during dinner (depending on the time of year and the time of sunset), so the photographer can capture those romantic, golden-hour shots.

Should You Have an Engagement Photo Session?

Some wedding photographers include an engagement photo shoot in one or more of their wedding packages, or they may offer it as an add-on service. Having your engagement session with the same photographers who will shoot your wedding gives you an extra opportunity to get to know them and get comfortable with them.

It can be somewhat awkward to have a professional photo shoot. You don't really know how to pose yourself, you don't know what to do with your hands, and you have to smile A LOT. If you do an engagement shoot with your wedding photographers, you'll already know them when your wedding day arrives, and you'll likely be more relaxed, which will show up in your photos.

There are wedding photographers who love to shoot weddings but don't love to shoot engagements. Those photographers generally either don't offer engagement shoots or they charge absurdly high rates for them, hoping to discourage couples from hiring them for an engagement shoot. So if you're considering a photographer and it seems like they charge an awful lot for an engagement shoot, they might fall into this camp. You can still hire them for your wedding, but feel free to look elsewhere for an engagement photographer.

You aren't required to use the same photographer for both your engagement shoot and your wedding day. You could book a photographer just for the engagement shoot as sort of a try-out. Maybe you'll then decide to also hire them for your wedding, or maybe you'll decide to go a different route.

Also consider having your engagement photos done while you're traveling somewhere fun. If you're going abroad, you can easily find a local photographer to do your shoot. They won't be the same photographer shooting your wedding (unless you want to pay for them to travel to do so), but it will certainly make for some memorable photos.

Social media makes finding a photographer really easy, even in cities you've never been to. Just search, for example, #newyorkcityengagement, #parisengagementphotos, #romeweddingphotographer, or similar to find accounts of photographers you can consider hiring.

What can you do with your engagement photos?

Save-the-Dates

One of the most popular uses for engagement photos is on save-the-date cards, sent out to your planned invitees well in advance of the wedding to let them know that they should mark that date off their calendars and start thinking about making travel plans, if necessary.

Save-the-date cards should be mailed fairly early — at least 9 months before a wedding taking place outside the country, and 6 months before a domestic wedding. Even if most of your guests won't have to travel to your wedding, you may want to send save-the-dates anyway.

If you want to use one or two engagement photos on your save-the-dates, you'll need to schedule the photo shoot 9-12 months before your wedding. You need time to schedule the shoot and have it, wait for the photographers to edit and send you the images, and then order and receive the save-the-dates. So prior planning is a must!

Wedding Website

Another popular use for engagement photos is on your wedding website. Your main page should have a nice photo of you and your fiancé(e), and you can also use them to tell your "story" as a couple. It's easy to sprinkle photos of yourselves throughout your wedding website, and some sites allow you to create an entire photo album online if you want to share all the photos.

Guest Book

Two fun ways to incorporate your engagement photos into your wedding day are to make an album and ask guests to sign the pages, or have a few photos custom matted and ask guests to sign the mat around the photos. Then you can frame your guest book and hang it on the wall in your home.

Even if you don't want to use the photos as your guest book, you can display a few framed engagement photos on your guest book table, so your guests can appreciate them.

Budget Concerns

If you really just don't have the budget to do an engagement photo shoot, then I recommend finding a friend or family member with a nice camera who knows how to use it. (By which I mean they know how to shoot in manual, they understand depth of field and the exposure triangle, and they have a good grasp of composition.) Ask them to do a mini-photo session with you. Being engaged is a special time, and you'll want to commemorate it in some way, even if it's not a full-blown engagement shoot.

How To Prepare for Your Engagement Photo Session

Choose Engagement Shoot Location

First you should choose the city in which you want to have your photos taken. This could be the city where you live, or a place nearby, or a completely different city. You could decide to travel elsewhere for the purpose of having your engagement photos taken, or you could do engagement photos in a city where you already have a trip planned.

If you live near, but not in, a large, famous city (like New York, San Francisco, Chicago, Los Angeles), you might want to consider having your engagement photo shoot in the larger city, especially if there's an iconic location in that city. Think of the Golden Gate Bridge, or Central Park.

Once you have the city chosen, you'll need to select an exact location. Maybe it's a spot that's special to you and your fiancé(e), or even the place where you got engaged. Some couples opt to do their engagement photos in their own home.

Your photographer may allow you to shoot at multiple locations, especially if they're reasonably close to each other. For example, in Washington D.C., many of the monuments and memorials are relatively close to each other at the National Mall. You could easily shoot some photos near the Washington Monument and then switch over to the Lincoln Memorial and the reflecting pool.

Check with your photographer to find out how many locations your shoot includes.

Choose Engagement Photo Outfits

Most engagement photos sessions are designed with one outfit change in mind (so, a total of two outfits). But check with your photographer to see if they can accommodate more than one outfit change. Outfit changes add time to the engagement session, so for an additional fee, your photographer may be willing to incorporate multiple outfit changes.

Your photographer may also send you a style guide to help you select the right type of outfits. If not, you can always snap a quick cell phone photo of the outfits you're considering and run them past your photographer.

Generally, you will want one dressy outfit and one casual outfit. You and your fiancé(e) want to complement each other without being matchy-matchy or clashing. Some patterns may not photograph well, which is why it's helpful to get your photographer's input. They should know what will look good in photos.

Footwear & Accessories

Be sure to consider terrain when choosing your shoes. If you're doing a beach photo shoot, you probably don't want to wear stilettos. If you'll be outside on uneven ground, it's wise to bring a pair of flats for getting into position. Then you can change into a wedge heel or something that won't sink into the ground for the actual photos.

Plan your jewelry and other accessories in advance as well. Watches, hats, scarves, jackets, or anything else you normally would accessorize with is fair game. But your engagement photos are probably not the place to experiment with a new look or style. You want the photos to be a reflection of you.

Photo Shoot Props

Think about any props you might want to use in your photos. Maybe you want to bring a picnic blanket and basket and stage a mock picnic. Maybe you want to have champagne flutes and some sparkling wine to do a toasting photo. If you plan to use your engagement photo on save-the-date cards, you might want some signage to hold up. "We're engaged!" or the date of your upcoming wedding are popular choices to put on the sign.

Instagram and Pinterest can be great sources of ideas and inspiration if you're trying to come up with ideas for cute photo ops.

Time of Day

Most photographers like to shoot during "golden hour"—the best light that happens the hour after sunrise and the hour before sunset. If you're planning your engagement shoot for the summer, sunrise might not be the best idea because it can be really early. You'll have a hard time finding someone to do your hair and makeup at 4 am.

Be prepared to take some time off work for your engagement photo shoot. Engagement photographers are usually also wedding photographers, which means they will be busy shooting weddings on the weekends and will want to schedule your engagement shoot for a weekday.

Primping for Your Engagement Photos

Ladies will probably want to have their hair and makeup professionally done for engagement photos. This is a perfect opportunity to try out a hair stylist and makeup artist for your wedding day. If you like the work they do for your engagement shoot, then you can be comfortable hiring them for your wedding.

Guys will want to have a haircut reasonably close to the day of the engagement photos. And if you want to be clean-shaven for the photos, you might need an afternoon shave just before the session, especially if you're subject to "five o'clock shadow."

Don't forget about your nails! Ladies may want a full manicure, and guys should at the very least make sure their cuticles are trimmed and their nails neatly filed. A gentlemen's manicure may be in order. It could be a fun couples' activity.

Lastly, be sure to clean your engagement ring just before the shoot. Your ring will be featured in some of the photos, and you want it to look its best.

Remember to relax and have fun! You will get tired of smiling, but it's good practice for your wedding day. And if you feel awkward or silly in the poses your photographer is asking you to do, just remember that they want you to look your best. Trust them and let them do their thing, and you'll get some fantastic photos out of it.

Your Homework Assignment

Spend some quality time on Instagram—QUALITY TIME, not mindless scrolling! Follow my tips above to search for wedding photographers in your area. Make a list of a few whose style you love. Google them and research their website. Remember, if they don't have a website, they're not taking their business seriously and they won't take your wedding seriously. Send inquiries and schedule consultations with your three favorite options.

Decide whether you want to do a first-look photo session, whether a second shooter makes sense for your wedding, and whether you want to do an engagement shoot. Discuss all of those with your potential photographers.

Use the Photographer Questionnaire to help you ask the right questions. Find the Photographer Questionnaire at www.risajamesevents.com/wedding-questionnaires.

Videographer

When you start planning your wedding, hiring a wedding photographer is a no-brainer, but what about hiring a wedding videographer? You might think you don't need or want one, or you might not have room in your current budget for one. But here are some reasons why you might want to hire a videographer, plus some tips for the wedding day to make your wedding video the best it can be.

Do You Need a Videographer and a Photographer?

Maybe you think wedding photos will be a sufficient memento of your wedding day, and maybe they will be. But if you're on the fence, here are a few reasons why you might want to consider having both a videographer and a photographer.

1. Wedding photos will help you remember the day, but a wedding video helps you *re-live* it. Photos capture a moment in time; video captures the scene as it unfolds.

2. A wedding photographer can't capture the sound of your vows being spoken or the sniffles of your parents during the ceremony.

3. A photographer can't truly capture all the epic dance moves going down on the dance floor, like your Best Man dancing with your grandma, or your cousin busting out the break-dancing.

4. Nothing can compare to sitting down with your loved ones and watching the entirety of your ceremony and speeches full-length, with all the crying and laughter in between. This is also a lovely anniversary tradition that you and your spouse can enjoy together. It's amazing to see all the little details that happen during a wedding that you don't see when you're in the middle of it. Only video can fully capture those for you.

Tips for Getting the Best Wedding Video

Once you've decided to hire a videographer, there are some things you can do to ensure that you get the best possible wedding video.

1. Spend some time talking about what you want with your videographer. A lot of planning goes into creating the perfect video. The more you have prepared ahead of time (versus just winging it on the wedding day), the better things will go. This is especially true if you and your

fiancé(e) are going to read letters to one another on video. Speaking off-the-cuff can be tricky. If you think about what you want to say ahead of time, and possibly write it down, you'll be much happier with the outcome.

2. When members of the wedding party get ready together, the room can get really messy. Videographers need room to move around to shoot different angles, and you don't want a pile of clothes or empty hangers in the background of your wedding video. Many videographers will try to clear away the clutter so they can get a good shot, but that's not why you're hiring them. You want them to spend their time shooting footage, not cleaning up your mess. Couples and their groomsmen/bridesmaids may want to pay attention to cleaning up as they go.

3. Some brides and grooms have a hard time putting away their cell phone on the wedding day, especially when getting ready. It's hard for your photo/video team to get a good shot when you're holding your phone. Passing your phone off to someone in your wedding party is a great way to ensure that you don't miss anything important, but also don't spend the morning of your wedding staring at your phone.

4. The couple should try to make sure the photographer and videographer have connected in advance so that they can coordinate and make sure they both have time to get the shots they need and there won't be any conflicts on the day of the wedding.

If you have a wedding planner or coordinator, that fourth point is definitely something they can help with. They are in communication with your wedding team, so they'll be sure to connect your photographer and videographer ahead of time so they can put their heads together and make sure each of them has the time they need to get the shots they want.

Your Homework Assignment

Discuss the importance of video with your partner and decide if you have room in your budget. If you do, follow the same path you took when searching for a photographer. Start on Instagram, move on to websites, send inquiries and schedule consultations with your top three options before selecting your video team.

Use the Videographer Questionnaire to help you ask the right questions. Find the Videographer Questionnaire at www.risajamesevents.com/wedding-questionnaires.

Caterer and bar service

Food and beverage are a huge part of any wedding, and this is the single most expensive line item in your budget. If your venue provides catering in-house, you will have fewer decisions to make, but there are still a lot of options for you to consider.

One of the biggest catering-related decisions you have to make is whether to have a buffet or a pre-plated meal. There are pros and cons to each approach.

Buffet Advantages

1. A buffet offers more options for your guests. You can do multiple meat options, a pasta course, and a vegetarian course. You can offer food stations — think made-for-you grilled cheese, baked potatoes with your choice of toppings, or a carving station with prime rib. You can do a sushi buffet, or a breakfast buffet for a morning wedding. The possibilities are practically endless.

2. With a buffet, no one will end up with food they don't like because they get to choose what goes on their plate.

3. Everyone gets to decide their own portions. Let's face it, some people eat more than others. Some people are dieting. Some are dealing with food restrictions. Giving people control over their portion sizes makes them happier.

4. It's easier for you. When you have a buffet, you don't have to put meal options on your response card or keep track of what everyone wants for dinner. You also don't need to make individual place cards indicating the guest's meal choice. Instead, you can make one large seating chart. Also, most caterers require assigned seats for a pre-plated meal, which means you have to make both escort cards (to tell people which table is theirs) AND place cards (to tell people which seat is theirs).

5. It could save you money on staff. Most caterers bring more staff members to serve a pre-plated meal table-side than they bring for a buffet. They still need staff to pour water and wine, to clear dishes, and to replenish the buffet chafing dishes, but it's generally not as many staff as are needed to serve table-side meals.

Pre-Plated Dinner Advantages

1. I'm not going to lie, a pre-plated meal served table-side is always going to be more elegant than a buffet. It's more like dining at a nice restaurant vs. dining at Golden Corral.

2. It can be easier to handle specific dietary restrictions with a pre-plated meal. If you know you have one (or several) gluten-free guests, it's easier to have just a few gluten-free meals to accommodate them than it is to make an entire buffet gluten-free. The same is true for guests who can't have dairy or soy. If you know you will have guests will food allergies, it's best to discuss with your caterer how to handle meal preparation.

You can take a hybrid approach to get some of the advantages of a buffet while still having a pre-plated meal. Serve multiple entrées on the same plate and give everyone the same two entrées (this is sometimes called "duet" service). You still don't have to include a meal choice on the response card or keep track of everyone's selections, but you get to give guests a little more choice and flexibility in what they eat.

Or serve family-style. Each table gets one or two large platters with the salad course, then more platters with the entrées and the sides. Guests can then serve themselves from the platters, but you still don't have to keep track of meal choices or assign seats to everyone.

Think about your overall vibe. If you want your wedding to be elegant and fancy, go with the pre-plated option served table-side. But if you're aiming for a more fun and relaxed vibe, then do a buffet or family-style.

The Catering "Service Charge" Explained

When you are reviewing catering quotes, there's one item that causes more trouble than anything else: the service charge. Catering quotes are generally made up of four components:

- the food (and drinks)
- staffing (chefs, captains, servers, bartenders)
- rentals (plates, flatware, glassware, linens, tables, chairs)
- taxes and fees

The "service charge" is found in the fourth category, taxes and fees. The service charge is generally a percentage of the total catering bill. It ranges from 10 percent to 20 percent, so if you are inviting a lot of people to your wedding, and your catering bill is high, your service charge is going to add on a significant amount of money.

Despite the word "service" being in the name, the service charge has nothing to do with the staff providing service at your wedding. It doesn't cover their labor, and it's not a gratuity for them either. If you decide to give the serving staff gratuities, that will be on top of the catering quote and invoice amount.

So what is the service charge, then? It's basically meant to cover the overhead and costs of doing business for the caterer. Restaurants and catering businesses run on very thin margins. That means that there's not much of a difference between what they charge and what their costs are. Food is expensive to buy, and it can be marked up only so much before it gets absurd.

Caterers have many other costs besides the food they buy to serve at your event. They have to have physical space—kitchens, commercial stoves and ovens, freezers, storage areas—which is expensive. Plus they need vehicles to transport all of the food and gear to your wedding location. And they need to buy and sometimes replace all that gear, like chafing dishes, serving utensils, serving dishes, etc. On top of that, they need administrative staff to handle all the bookings and prepare all the quotes. In order to cover those costs, they add on the service charge to their bookings.

It's important to keep in mind that when you review a sample menu or a list of catering packages, the prices you're seeing (usually listed as a per person price) are for FOOD ONLY. The staffing, rentals, taxes, and service charge are not yet included.

This is why it's very important that you get a full quote from multiple caterers to compare before making your final decision. Don't decide based only on their sample menus. You will be underestimating the total catering cost by a pretty wide margin if you do.

The catering service charge is widely misunderstood, and not explained very well by the catering industry. Just remember (and this goes for all contracts you enter into), if there's a fee or a charge you don't understand, ask about it. Don't be afraid of looking uninformed. You have the right to understand what you're paying for.

Wedding Bar Options

When it comes to your wedding bar and the type of alcohol you serve, you have several options: full bar, beer + wine + signature cocktails, beer & wine only, or no alcohol at all. Let's examine these one by one, beginning with the easiest and working our way up to the most complicated.

Option 1: Serve no alcohol at all

This option is really only common among some religious groups, such as Muslims, who abstain from alcohol altogether. In these cases, most of the guests are probably also of the same religion, and it's fine to not serve alcohol. Some guests might even be offended if alcohol is available.

The no-alcohol approach is not recommended if most of your guests are drinkers but you and your fiancé(e) are not. In that case, as a gracious host, you will still want to have some alcoholic beverages available. Let's be honest: weddings are more fun and entertaining when people have a little alcohol. Not to the point where things get out of hand, but enough to ensure a good time. Your guests are more likely to dance and have fun after a drink or two.

Option 2: Beer & wine only

This is a great option if you are on a tight budget. Beer and wine are less expensive than liquor, and there are ways to stretch your budget further if you're providing the alcohol yourself. (More on that later.)

With beer, you can get more bang for your buck (or "beer for your buck," if you will) by purchasing kegs. You just have to be careful with quantities, because you don't want to have beer left in the keg at the end of the night. You also need to be sure that your venue/caterer/bartender has the capability of serving from kegs. They do require some special equipment, and also space.

Wine can be purchased in large-format bottles called magnums, which hold 1.5 liters of wine (as opposed to a standard bottle of wine, which is 750 ml). Each magnum will provide 10 glasses of wine, and it can be more economical to purchase wine by the magnum. Keep in mind though that not all wine is bottled in magnums, so your options might be limited there.

Option 3: Beer + wine + signature cocktails

Signature cocktails are a great way to incorporate some liquor into your wedding bar without going crazy and breaking the bank. In most cases, the couple will choose two signature cocktails: a "his and hers" or "groom's and bride's." (Or "hers and hers" or "his and his," depending on the couple. For same-sex couples, I actually recommend using each partner's name for the signature cocktail to avoid confusion.)

The signature cocktail allows you to personalize your wedding and share your favorite cocktail with your guests. If you want to give your guests a bit more variety, you can do as many as four signature cocktails. If your venue has restrictions on liquor, you might have to limit yourselves to just one signature cocktail. This is a question to ask during the venue tour if the bar is important to you.

Option 4: Full bar

This option gives your guests the most options when it comes to drinking. But it's also the most complicated for you to put together if you're bringing in all the alcohol to your wedding venue, and it's the most expensive option.

Imagine having to purchase and bring in vodka, gin, tequila, mezcal, Irish whiskey, Scotch whisky, Tennessee whiskey, Bourbon, Canadian whisky, cognac, brandy and more. Not to mention all the necessary mixers and fruit garnishes. And if you want to offer more than one brand of gin or vodka, well that all starts to add up fast!

A full bar only makes sense if you are getting married in a venue that provides the catering and bar service in-house: a hotel, a country club, or some other sort of inclusive venue. They already have all the liquor in stock and available. Your guests can order what they want, and the venue will simply charge you based on consumption. You can choose to serve premium spirits or entry-level spirits. You don't have to guess in advance what people are going to want to drink. And you don't have to worry about having too much or too little of any particular liquor.

Service Options

Besides choosing what type of alcohol to serve at your wedding, you also have to figure out how it will be served, and by whom.

If your wedding venue is a hotel, country club, or other inclusive venue, you don't have to do much of anything. They provide all the liquor, wine, beer, mixers, garnishes, ice, cocktail napkins, and drink stirrers, plus the staff to serve.

All you have to do is decide which level of spirits you want to offer your guests. "Well" is the entry-level brand. "Call" is the next step up. "Premium" is the top-shelf brand. The venue will give you examples of which brands fall into each level. Prices per drink will be higher for "call" and highest for "premium."

If you've hired a full-service caterer (meaning they set your tables, provide food and waitstaff, and clean up at the end of the night), they probably can also provide bar services. In some cases, they will provide all the alcohol and charge you per drink or per bottle. Or you might be able to provide the alcohol, and they will provide the staff. Check with both your caterer and your venue if you want to provide the alcohol yourself—some of them have limitations on this.

If you're providing all the alcohol, they may also want you to provide all the mixers and garnishes as well, or they might have a discounted price for those items. You can definitely save money by buying your own alcohol, even if you're paying retail price for it. But it can be worth your time and money to pay the caterers to provide the mixers and garnishes. It's definitely worth it for them to provide the ice, if they will. See the note below.

If your caterer does not provide bar services, you can hire bartenders separately. Many rental companies have bar structures that you can rent for your wedding.

When you hire separate bartenders, it's often expected that you will provide everything they need: all the alcohol, mixers, garnishes, and ice. Mobile bars have also become popular the past couple of years. These are usually old horse trailers that have been refurbished and turned into bars. They are known as "dry hire" bars, meaning they provide service but you provide the alcohol.

A note about ice

If at all possible, have your bartenders or caterers provide the ice. You need a ridiculous amount of ice for a wedding. The rule of thumb is 1–2 pounds per guest, depending on the time of year and how hot it will be. So if you're having 150 guests at your wedding, you need 150–300 pounds of ice. That's 30–60 five-pound bags. It's a lot.

Ice is used in many cocktails, but it's also used to chill white wines, sparkling wine, beer, soda, and water. You need a lot of ice to fill those buckets or tubs. If you're getting married outdoors in the summer, the ice will melt quickly and have to be replenished often. Always, always buy more ice than you think you will need.

A big wedding bar no-no

Whatever option you choose, do NOT, under any circumstances, have a cash bar. This is completely socially unacceptable. You've invited people to be your guests at your wedding. You wouldn't charge them for their dinner. Why would you charge them for alcohol? If budget is a concern, serve less alcohol (cut out the signature cocktails, or limit the times for the bar) or invite fewer people. But do not charge people who come to your wedding. Just don't.

Deciding What to Serve

Liquor

If you want to serve liquor at your wedding, the easiest and most cost-effective way to do it is to choose some signature cocktails. As explained above, serving signature cocktails allows you to incorporate cocktails into your wedding bar without the trouble and expense of having a full bar.

Another advantage to signature cocktails is that they allow you, as the couple, to personalize your wedding. Everyone wants their wedding to reflect their personalities, and sharing your favorite drinks with your guests is an easy way to do that.

Usually the signature cocktails are the only cocktails available at the wedding. You can do signature cocktails as part of a full bar, but guests are less likely to drink the signature cocktails if they can get anything they want at the bar. And you've undermined some of the advantages of signature cocktails by adding them onto a full bar, rather than having them stand alone.

How to choose your signature cocktails

Start with your favorite cocktail, if you have one. Is there something you're known for drinking? Do you have a go-to bar order when out with friends? Is there a particular drink that played a part in your first date or your engagement?

If you don't have a particular favorite drink, do you have a favorite liquor? Some people love whiskey but not vodka. Some are big tequila drinkers. Again, one of the reasons to have signature cocktails is to personalize your wedding, so think about what you like.

Which liquors to use

It's best to have cocktails with different base spirits. I recommend one clear liquor (vodka, gin, white rum, tequila *blanco*) and one brown liquor (whiskey, bourbon, dark rum, tequila *reposado*).

Another consideration is the sweetness level of the drinks. If you're serving a bourbon cocktail or something with St. Germain in it, both of which are on the sweet side, then consider something more herbaceous and bitter as the counterpart. For example, an Old-Fashioned (sweet, and made with whiskey) and a Negroni (bitter, and made with gin). Or a Moscow Mule (made with vodka, ginger beer, and lots of ice) and a Margarita (more spirit-forward than a Moscow Mule because it doesn't have a fizzy component).

Time of year matters

Also keep in mind the time of year. If it's the middle of summer and likely to be hot, you'll want your cocktails to skew toward the refreshing spectrum. Think: mojito, Tom Collins, or whiskey highball. If it's autumn, you can skew toward the heavier end of the cocktail spectrum with an Old-Fashioned, Dark & Stormy, or Moscow Mule.

Time of year applies to garnishes as well. You don't want to serve something with an apple garnish in May or June when apples are out of season. The same goes for berries. Pinterest is a real problem in this regard. You may fall in love with the look of a drink, but it may be all wrong for your particular wedding.

Don't overcomplicate things

You also want to keep your cocktails on the simple side. Anything too elaborate will be difficult for your bartenders to make quickly. Drinks that can be pre-batched are always winners. Your bartenders, caterers, or wedding planner can help you choose wisely if you're having trouble.

If you want to keep the bar limited, but you want to offer more options than just two cocktails, you can choose two spirits plus a variety of mixers and let your guests have more leeway with their cocktail orders. For example, vodka, whiskey, soda water, tonic water, ginger beer, cranberry juice, simple syrup, lemon juice, lime juice, and a few different fruit garnishes will give your bartenders a lot of flexibility with creating drinks.

Popular signature cocktail choices

The Old-Fashioned is hands-down the most popular signature cocktail choice. It's fairly easy to make, doesn't require a lot of ingredients, and most people have heard of it. A French 75 is another popular choice. Gin & Champagne — what's not to love?

Other popular options include the Greyhound, Paloma, Manhattan, Moscow Mule, Dark & Stormy, Margarita, and Cosmopolitan. In my city of Sacramento, the White Linen is hugely popular, because it was invented by one of our local bartenders.

Wine

Unless you're having an alcohol-free wedding, chances are good that you will be serving wine. So how do you choose which wines to serve at your wedding? As with most things wedding-related, always start with what you like. It is your wedding, after all. You want to consider your guests and their experience as well, but thinking about what you and your partner like is a great way to get started.

At a minimum, you'll want to have one white wine option and one red wine option. It's even better if you add on a rosé and a sparkling option. The next step up from there would be two whites, two reds, one rosé, and a sparkling. More than that might be overwhelming for your guests.

Food & Wine Pairings

If you already know what foods will be served at your wedding, both during cocktail hour and at dinner, that can guide your wine choices. The most basic rule of thumb when pairing food and wine is that white foods go with white wine and dark foods go with red wine. So white wine for seafood, chicken, and pork. Red wine for beef.

But not so fast! Because salmon, which is obviously seafood, is actually best paired with Pinot Noir, which is a red wine. And there are a lot of lighter-bodied, fruit-forward red wines that will go well with chicken or pork. Sauces also matter. Richer sauces require a more full-bodied wine to cut through them.

Don't be overwhelmed though. Your bartender, caterer, or wedding planner can help you navigate wine and food pairings.

Which Type of Wines to Serve

When it comes to varietals (that is, what kind of wine), you can go with very common, well-known wines or choose more unusual, interesting wines.

White Wine Options

Common whites include Chardonnay and Sauvignon Blanc. Most people are familiar with those wines and know whether or not they like them.

Chardonnay is generally a full-bodied wine with a rich mouthfeel. It tastes "round" and "soft" when you drink it. Chardonnays that have been aged in American oak barrels can sometimes be described as "buttery." Chardonnay is a great match for cheeses, cream sauces on pasta, and lighter white meats like chicken and pork.

Sauvignon Blanc is a more astringent, high-acid wine that can be citrusy or grassy in its flavor profile. Sauvignon Blanc is an excellent pairing for seafoods such as scallops, shrimp, white fish, mollusks, and bi-valves. It's crisp and can be almost tart.

If you wanted to choose a less-common, more unusual white, you could go with a Chenin Blanc (from France or South Africa) or a Pinot Grigio from Italy instead of Chardonnay. Assyrtiko from Greece would be an excellent substitution for Sauvignon Blanc.

Red Wine Options

On the red side, the most common options are Cabernet Sauvignon, Merlot, and Pinot Noir. Cabernet Sauvignon and Merlot tend toward the heavier end of the spectrum. They are generally more tannic and powerful. (Tannins come from the grape skins and are the element of wine that makes your tongue feel kind of dry, like you just rubbed cotton on it.)

Pinot Noir is a lighter-bodied red wine, and generally a bit more fruit-forward than either Cabernet Sauvignon or Merlot. Pinot Noir from California often has a lot of cherry flavor to it, while Pinots from France or Oregon are a little fuller, with some elements of earth, mushroom, and tobacco. But even a more full-bodied Pinot Noir is lighter than a Cabernet Sauvignon or a Merlot.

If you want to go off the beaten path with your red choices, you could do a Beaujolais instead of Pinot Noir. By "Beaujolais" I don't mean the Beaujolais Nouveau that you usually see in the wine stores around Thanksgiving. Those are very fresh, extremely fruit-forward wines made from grapes harvested mere weeks before bottling. The Beaujolais region of France also makes more traditional wines that are aged some number of months before release. They are labeled Beaujolais or Beaujolais Villages.

Instead of Cabernet Sauvignon or Merlot, you could try Chianti (an Italian varietal), Tempranillo (a Spanish varietal), or a GSM. GSM stands for Grenache, Syrah, Mourvèdre. Those grape varieties are all grown in the Rhône Valley in Southern France, and GSM is a typical Rhône blend.

One reason many people choose the more familiar varietals is that you can find inexpensive versions of those wines a little more easily than you can find inexpensive versions of the lesser-known wines. Also, if you decide to serve more unusual wines, you'll want to give the bar staff or waitstaff some notes to describe the wines. It's likely that your guests will ask them what those wines are like or what they compare to.

Champagne & Sparkling Wine

When it comes to sparkling wine, you also have several options. Champagne is the most famous (and most expensive) type of sparkling wine. Technically, a wine can only be called Champagne if it's made in the Champagne region of France. It's typically made from Chardonnay, Pinot Noir, and/or Pinot Meunier grapes using a traditional method that goes back centuries. Champagne generally ranges in price from $40 to $200 per bottle, so unless you have a small guest list and a large budget, it may not be the best choice for your wedding.

California sparkling wine is made primarily with the same grapes using the same process as Champagne, but is more reasonably priced. You can find good bottles of California sparkling wine for $15 to $40 per bottle.

Prosecco and Cava are Italian and Spanish, respectively, sparkling wines. They are made using indigenous grapes (meaning, grapes that are native to those countries and don't really grow elsewhere). Some prosecco and cava are made using the traditional Champagne method, but most are made using a less labor- and time-intensive process, which is why they cost less. You can find good prosecco and cava for $8 to $20 per bottle.

Champagne and sparkling wines are excellent food wines. They pair with pretty much everything. The bubbles and high acidity make them very food friendly; plus, they have a celebratory feel that is highly appropriate for a wedding. Consider making sparkling wine available throughout the night, not just for the toasts.

Rosé

Rosé is another food-friendly option. Without going too far down the rabbit hole, rosé is made one of two ways. Either a bit of red wine is blended together with a white wine, or the wine is made with just a little bit of skin contact to give it some light red color. All grapes are clear on the inside, so their juice is clear. The color is in the grape skins.

After grapes are picked, they are crushed to release the juices. If the skins and juice are immediately separated, the resulting wine will be white. If the juice is allowed to sit with the skins for a period of time (called maceration), the resulting wine will be red. To get a lighter pink or rose color, the skins are left with the juice for a short period of time. Not long enough to make the wine red; just long enough to get a bit of the color.

Along with the color comes some depth of flavor and maybe even a little bit of tannin, which is what makes rosé wines so food-friendly. Plus, rosé has been having a bit of a moment the past few years—#roséallday anyone? No one will be sorry to see rosé on your wedding drinks menu.

Consider Time of Year

As with signature cocktails, consider the time of year when choosing your wines. If your wedding is being held in the hot summer months, you'll want more whites and rosé on hand. Those wines are served chilled and are very refreshing. (They are also lower in alcohol than red wines, so people can drink more without getting drunk.)

In colder months, you'll want to skew more toward red wines. The higher alcohol content and slightly warmer serving temperature tends to warm people up a bit, rather than cooling them off.

Where to Buy Wines

If you are providing the wines yourself for your wedding, you'll want to find the best prices. Costco and Sam's Club can be cost-effective places to buy wine. They buy in bulk, so they can pass lower prices onto you. However, their selections will be limited.

Total Wine, BevMo, and other "big box" wine retailers are another great option if you have one near where you live. Total Wine has a wedding service that allows you to schedule a tasting appointment. They'll sit down with you, taste a variety of wines, provide education, and help you make your selections. This is a fantastic option for you DIYers out there.

If you live in a strict liquor control state, I'm afraid you're stuck with whatever selections and prices your local state store offers. Ask your caterer, bartender, or planner for some suggestions.

If you live near wineries and can visit to do an in-person tasting, this can be a great way to find wines for your wedding. Most wineries will be happy to negotiate a discounted price for you if you're going to buy multiple cases of wine to serve at a wedding. All you have to do is ask!

The world of wine is vast. There are so many great options for your wedding.

How to Know How Much Alcohol to Buy

If you will be directly purchasing the alcohol for your wedding, you'll want to know how much to buy. Your caterer or bar manager should be able to help you figure this out, but if you want to do it yourself, there are a few online calculators that can help. My favorite online calculator is https://www.liquordepot.ca/Party-Planner/Drink-Calculator. You enter the number of guests, the length of the event, and the percentage of people you think will drink wine, beer, or liquor.

Keep in mind that the length of the event does not include the ceremony because the bar (usually) doesn't open until after the ceremony. The bar also usually closes 30 to 60 minutes before the end of the reception. Last call is determined by your venue's policies.

Your Homework Assignment

If you chose a venue with in-house catering, your work is done for now. Eventually you will need to make menu selections, but that can wait until the venue reaches out to schedule a tasting.

If you're hiring an independent caterer, start by reviewing your venue's preferred list. Research caterers online and schedule phone consultations with a few. Tasting appointments generally have a fee, which may or may not be applied to any minimum fees required by the caterer when you book them for your wedding.

Discuss bar service with your potential caterers. Most can provide bar services as well. If you're interested in a specific type of bar service (mobile craft cocktail bar, multiple beer kegs, a trained sommelier for wine service), you'll want to engage the services of a specialty company. Use the same approach as for other service providers: start by asking friends or your coordinator for recommendations, research online, schedule consultations, then make a decision.

Use the Caterer and Bar Service Questionnaires to help you ask the right questions. Find the Caterer and Bar Service Questionnaires at www.risajamesevents.com/wedding-questionnaires.

Decide whether you want to serve a full bar or one of the other options described above. Then narrow down your exact selections as you get closer to the wedding date and once you've finalized your menu with your caterer.

Entertainment

Choosing the right entertainment for your wedding is a BIG DEAL. Music sets the mood and energy level. The first thing you should do is think about other weddings you've attended and what their entertainment was like (and whether you enjoyed it).

Ask yourself what kind of vibe you're looking for. Do you want your wedding to feel like an elegant dinner party? Then maybe a jazz combo would be the right fit. Do you want to throw a raucous blow-out bash? Consider a band. Do you have eclectic musical tastes ranging from classic rock to '80s pop to hip-hop? A versatile DJ will be your best bet.

There are three components of an afternoon or evening wedding: ceremony, cocktail hour, and reception. If you are having a morning or brunch wedding, you only have two components: ceremony and reception. You can have the same entertainment provider for the entire wedding, or you can hire different musicians for different components.

If you are getting married in a house of worship, you will almost certainly need separate ceremony musicians. DJ and band set-ups are complicated and can take up to two hours to fully assemble. Not only would they logistically not be able to set up in the ceremony and reception space at the same time, but they would be very inappropriate in a religious setting.

Many churches have organists who play for regular services. If you're a member of the congregation and you know and like the organist, consider hiring her or him for your wedding. You may also consider a string quartet or harpist. Some churches limit the type of music that can be played to hymns or other liturgical songs. Be sure to check with your clergy for restrictions.

Even if you are not planning to hold your ceremony in a house of worship, you may still wish to hire separate ceremony musicians. String or brass quartets, jazz trios, and harpists are all popular choices. Often these musicians will also play during cocktail hour and then depart, with the DJ or band taking over entertainment duties for the rest of the evening. Most live musicians have a minimum amount of time that you need to book them, and it's often two hours. So to make the most of your budget, you'll want them to play for half an hour before the ceremony starts, during the ceremony, and during cocktail hour.

You might be tempted to use an iPhone or other device to play music through a sound system for some or all of your wedding. I recommend against this for several reasons. First, if something goes wrong, there's no one to fix it. Even if you assign a friend to be in charge of the device, problems with the sound system would be out of their control. Second, venue sound systems are often nowhere near as powerful as the system a band or DJ would provide.

You may not be able to hear the music over the din of the crowd. Third, if you intend to have dancing at your wedding, nothing compares to having a live person controlling what is played and for how long. Bands and DJs are experienced in reading a crowd and responding accordingly with their musical selections. You lose all of that personal touch using a pre-loaded device.

Band vs. DJ

If you're not sure whether you want a band or a DJ, here are a few points of comparison for you to consider.

- Price: bands are generally more expensive than DJs.
- Flexibility: bands usually have a particular style or repertoire, whereas DJs have more versatility in what they can play.
- Packages: DJs often have packages that include ceremony music, microphones for the ceremony and for toasting during the reception, and sometimes even lighting. Bands are more likely to play a shorter set and provide fewer accessories or extras.
- Meals: bands have multiple people that you have to feed during the reception. DJs generally have only one or two people.
- Breaks: most DJs don't take scheduled breaks. They can program a few songs to play during dinner so they can eat. Bands will have one or two scheduled breaks during their set; possibly more, depending on how long they're scheduled to play. They usually will provide pre-recorded music to play during their breaks.
- Volume: bands are LOUD. If your wedding is taking place indoors, I recommend a DJ instead. A band will make it impossible for anyone at your wedding to have a conversation. If you are holding your wedding outside and want to have a band, don't have them play during dinner. Either hire a DJ for dinner, or ask the band to play pre-recorded music. Save the band's energy (and noise) for the dance party.

Alternate wedding entertainment

If you aren't much of a dancer and don't really want to have music-centric entertainment, there are quite a few alternatives to consider.

Low-Key Music

Your DJ can still be deeply involved in your reception entertainment, even if they aren't playing the typical high-energy dance music. They usually play low-key music during dinner anyway, so that can continue past dinner. Rather than a wedding reception like we've all been to, your wedding would be more like a dinner party.

Games

Some DJs and MCs have a repertoire of games that they incorporate into their weddings, usually during dinner. If that's something that interests you, talk to your DJ about doing the games after dinner, in lieu of dancing. You and your new spouse might also want to play the "shoe game." You sit back-to-back on the dance floor and each of you holds one of your own shoes and one of your partner's shoes. The DJ or a guest asks a series of "Who?" questions, such as, "Who said I love you first?" or "Who snores the loudest?" You then each hold up a shoe with your answer, and it's entertaining for your guests to see if your answers match.

Live Musicians

Instead of hiring a DJ, maybe you want to hire live musicians to play. It's more entertaining for people to watch musicians play than it is to watch a DJ push buttons. You could hire a string quartet for your ceremony and cocktail hour, and then a jazz trio or a brass section for dinner and post-dinner.

This is a great option if you still want to do a first dance and maybe dances with your parents, but you don't want a full-on party dance floor.

Non-Musical Entertainment

Some of these ideas can veer too far into "child's birthday party" if not done well, but they're still entertaining. Consider hiring a mentalist or magician. Mentalists mostly stick to asking questions and then divining information about the audience. Magicians, on the other hand, typically perform card tricks and similar illusions.

Artists are another non-musical option. You can hire a portraitist to sketch quick portraits of couples or small friend groups. Or even a caricaturist, if that's to your liking.

One of my favorite art-related ideas is to hire an artist to live-paint a scene from the wedding. This works best if you want them to paint a scene from the ceremony, because it happens early on in the wedding. The artist paints a little background work before the ceremony, then paints live during the moment, and then fills in details throughout the rest of the evening. Your guests can check in on its progress at various times, and then at the end of the night, you could do a big reveal of the final painting. Bonus: you now have an amazing piece of custom art for your home.

And my last suggestion is something that is safe only if you're having an outdoor wedding: hire a fire dancer! Your guests will never forget that entertainment.

Your Homework Assignment

Decide on whether you want a DJ or a band (or something else) for the reception. If you're going with a band, you'll probably need separate musicians for the ceremony. If you go with a DJ, they can easily provide ceremony music as well, or you can hire live musicians for ceremony and cocktail hour. Research your options using the framework we've used before: recommendations, online research, consultations.

Use the Ceremony Musicians and DJ/Band Questionnaires to help you ask the right questions. Find the Ceremony Musicians and DJ/Band Questionnaires at www.risajamesevents.com/wedding-questionnaires.

After meeting with 1–3 DJs or bands, make a decision.

Florist and décor

Unless you throw a lot of very fancy dinner parties, your wedding is likely the first time you've ever had to hire a florist. You may have no idea where to start when it comes to deciding on floral décor for your wedding. Even if you already know what kind of flowers you want, there are some other practical concerns to address when hiring a florist.

Stylistic Considerations

Getting started is as easy as thinking about your favorite flowers. Maybe you're a huge fan of peonies, or roses are your go-to. You can also rule out flowers that you don't like. Some people love gerbera daisies, others not so much.

What's your color palette? You'll want florals to coordinate or complement your overall color scheme. But don't worry, there are flowers in every color. And you can combine different shades of the same color by using different flowers.

You should also think about whether you want formal structured arrangements, or a more natural "just-picked" style. Pinterest and Instagram can be great sources of inspiration for florals because they are visual media. You can find some florists to check out and get a sense of what the various styles look like. See what appeals to you.

I recommend creating a Pinterest board (or a saved collection on Instagram) for flowers and just pinning things you like without overthinking it. Once you've collected about 30–40 pins, you can step back and evaluate your choices and look for commonalities. Did you pin a lot of very tall, structured arrangements? Did you love a bunch of long garland centerpieces? Patterns will begin to emerge, and then you'll know what kind of style you like.

Another reason to check out florists on Instagram is that many of them don't have the greatest websites. By looking at Instagram, you can get a good sense of their past work and what they're capable of creating.

Practical Considerations

Once you've found a few florists whose style you like, it's time to schedule some consultations. It's helpful to bring some examples of work you like to help guide your floral designer. But be sure to stay open to their ideas as well. After all, this is their craft and they are likely to have great suggestions. The questionnaire at the back of this book has a full list of questions to ask your potential florist.

Before your floral consultation, it's worthwhile to spend a bit of time thinking about how many and what type of florals you will need for your wedding. This comprehensive list will be a good starting point for you.

Personal Flowers

These are all the florals that are worn or carried by the people in your wedding. Obviously this changes a little bit if there are two brides or two grooms, but this will give you a general idea.

1. Bride: bouquet & tossing bouquet (a smaller version of the bride's primary bouquet).

2. Maid of Honor and Bridesmaids: maybe you want the maid of honor bouquet to be a little different than the bridesmaids' bouquets. Sometimes it's a little larger, and sometimes it has different flowers in it. Usually the bridesmaids' bouquets have similar flowers to the bride's bouquet, but maybe they are a different color.

3. Flower girls: will they wear flower crowns? Carry floral wands or posies? Toss loose petals out of baskets?

4. Corsages: generally for the mothers and grandmothers, but can also be for sisters or other special family members you want to honor. Keep in mind that corsages can be worn either on the wrist or pinned onto the dress. Check with each person who will be wearing a corsage to see what their preference is. Some dresses are very delicate and will not be appropriate for a pinned corsage.

5. Boutonnières: groom, best man, groomsmen, ring bearer(s), fathers, grandfathers, other special family members, and potentially your officiant.

Table Centerpieces

1. Each dinner table should have some sort of centerpiece arrangement. A standard round table seats 8-10 people. Eight is comfortable; ten is a little snug. Divide your total guest list by 8 or 10 to get an estimate of how many tables you will have. This number will change once you get your RSVPs in and finalize the guest list, but for an initial consultation, an estimate will do.

2. Don't forget about the sweetheart table or head table. The head table is usually a set of long, rectangular tables where the couple sits in the middle with their wedding party members out to each side. The sweetheart table is a small table where the couple sits by themselves.

3. With a head table, you may want to do multiple centerpieces or a long garland. Keep in mind that your bridesmaids will have bouquets. You can put empty vases filled with water on the head table and ask the bridesmaids to put their bouquets in the vases to take the place of centerpieces.

4. If your sweetheart table is round, a small centerpiece is a nice fit. If you're at a rectangular sweetheart table, a garland draping across the table and down the sides makes a dramatic impact.

Accent Arrangements

There are a lot of tables in and around your reception space besides the dinner tables. Signage also sometimes benefits from a bit of floral emphasis.

1. Welcome sign: maybe a small sprig at the top or on one corner.
2. Entryway or foyer: consider two tall arrangements, or arrangements on pillars, flanking the entrance.
3. Guest book/gift table.
4. Escort card table or sign: with a sign, a small sprig like on the welcome sign dresses it up just a bit more. If you're doing tented escort cards on a round table, a statement centerpiece in the middle is eye-catching upon entry.
5. Favor table display.
6. Beverage station/bar/bar menu: if you're offering cold beverages before a summer ceremony or hot beverages before an autumn ceremony, dress up the station with an arrangement. The bar menu can also benefit from a sprig of florals.
7. Buffet tables: check with your caterer to see if they have standard décor they use. Buffet tables are often pretty crowded with chafing dishes and serving utensils. They generally don't need a lot of adornment.
8. Cake & cake table: whether or not you have fresh flowers on your cake, you may want some loose petals for the table or to place around the base of the cake.

Ceremony Flowers

1. Ceremony arch: you will certainly want to dress it up with some combination of a fabric drape and a floral display. Often we use more greenery on the arch because it's a lot of real estate to cover, and flowers are expensive. If you can find a place to re-purpose the arch display (say, on the sweetheart table), you can get more bang for your buck.
2. If you don't have a ceremony arch (or even if you do), you can place two large arrangements on either side of the ceremony space to designate it. This is another good place for arrangements on pillars.

3. The aisle: consider lining it with loose rose petals, or drape fabric swags between each chair and hang arrangements off the side of the chairs lining the aisle.

4. Loose petals or lavender to toss. Check with your venue to see if they allow this and whether there's a clean-up fee.

Thinking about all of these possibilities before your consultation allows you to have a more productive meeting and get a more accurate floral quote from your florist.

Your Homework Assignment

Using the framework that should be familiar to you by now, make a list of a few potential floral designers whose work you like. Send inquiries about availability and schedule consultations with your top three. If a florist's inquiry form has a LOT of questions, that's usually a sign that they are expensive and are trying to weed out inquiries that aren't serious.

You're unlikely to find any pricing on a florist's website because their pricing depends heavily on your choices—what type of flowers you want, whether they're in season, how many arrangements you need, how large you want them to be, etc. Some florists have a minimum amount, so that's a great question to ask up front. If their minimum exceeds your budget, cross them off and move on until you find the right fit.

One caveat about florists' websites: some of them are horrendous. Don't ask me why, but I've seen more than one that looks like it hasn't been updated since 1999. It's not necessarily a reflection on the florist's design work, because I've worked with some extremely talented florists who have terrible websites. So don't let that be a deal-breaker for you. Looking at photos of their past work is the best way to gauge their design skills, so if they don't have a great website, ask them to send you a portfolio over email.

Use the Florist Questionnaire to help you ask the right questions. Find the Florist Questionnaire at www.risajamesevents.com/wedding-questionnaires.

Stationer or calligrapher

Invitations

There are a lot of options when it comes to your wedding invitations and save-the-dates. Anywhere you can order printed holiday cards probably also does wedding invitations. Online invitation sources make some lovely options in any possible design you could want. But if you want a truly one-of-a-kind invitation suite, you'll want to hire a stationer to create something for you.

You'll need several items in your invitation suite: save-the-date cards, the invitation itself (with an envelope), a response card (with an envelope), and possibly a directions insert or an invitation to the rehearsal dinner or post-wedding brunch. You also probably want thank you cards in a matching design. If you opt for online responses, you won't need the paper response card and envelope. We'll talk more about invitations and save-the-dates, along with signage, in the next chapter.

Invitation Addressing

When the time comes to address your wedding invitations, you basically have three options: computer-generated, handwritten, or professional calligraphy. Your invitation sets the tone for your wedding. Only you can decide what you want that tone to be.

I don't recommend computer-generated envelope addressing if you're doing it yourself. Thanks to the near impossibility of getting your home printer to accurately print onto specialty envelopes, it requires the use of stick-on labels. Those are fine for holiday cards and children's birthday parties, not for your wedding. If your stationer or invitation provider offers the option of pre-addressing the invitation envelopes (much like they print the return address on the envelope flap and the mailing address on the response card envelope), that can be an easy route to elegance.

Hand-writing the mailing addresses on your wedding invitations lends a nice personal touch (and has the added advantage of being extremely low-cost), if you have nice penmanship or know someone who does. Depending on the size of your guest list though, this could be a daunting, time-consuming task. Unless you are truly in a budget crunch, I don't recommend it if you're sending more than 50 invitations.

The most elegant option, of course, is to hire a professional calligrapher. When a large, ornately addressed envelope arrives in a mailbox, the recipient knows it contains something special. Calligraphy can be rather expensive, but if you have room in your budget and want to give your invitations that something special, professional calligraphy is the way to go. Calligraphers often charge by the line, so if your guest list includes a lot of apartment-dwellers, be aware that this will increase the total cost.

If you would like to feature calligraphy as part of your wedding but can't afford to have the invitations addressed, you can have your escort cards calligraphed, or have one master menu calligraphed and then reproduced by a local print shop. And if you decide to have the invitations calligraphed, have one addressed to yourself as a keepsake and also so your photographer can capture it when they photograph your stationery suite.

Your wedding day is likely to be the fanciest day of your life. It's only fitting that the writing should be fancy too.

Your Homework Assignment

With your color scheme, venue, and time of year in mind, start browsing invitation websites such as Minted, Basic Invite, and Shutterfly. You can filter by a number of criteria to narrow down your options. Be sure to create an account and log in so you can save your favorites.

If you don't see what you want on one of the large sites, consider having a suite custom-made. As usual, Instagram can be helpful here, but Google might be more helpful, thanks to location tagging. You can search hashtags on Instagram, but you might have a hard time finding a local stationer. Because Google knows where you live, searching for "custom wedding invitations" will automatically pull up local options. Your wedding coordinator or venue may also be able to make recommendations.

Remember that save-the-dates should be sent 6–9 months before the wedding, and it can take 8–10 days to receive your stationery after placing an order online. So be sure to choose an invitation design early in the wedding planning process. If you are going the custom route, the delivery time will be much longer than with an online service.

We'll talk more about invitations and wording, along with signage in Chapter 5.

If you decide to hire a calligrapher for either invitations, envelope addressing, or signage, use the Calligrapher Questionnaire to help you ask the right questions. Find the Calligrapher Questionnaire at www.risajamesevents.com/wedding-questionnaires.

Bakery

If you are planning to have a cake at your wedding, you will invariably find yourself at a cake tasting appointment at some point during your planning process. These tips will help you have a more productive meeting and provide some general cake-related knowledge.

Do a little cake research

As with all things wedding-related, it's helpful if you go to your meeting having some idea of what you want. There are so many options when it comes to cake design that you need to narrow the field a bit. Pinterest and wedding magazines are your friends here.

Find cakes that appeal to you and pin them to a wedding cake board on Pinterest. Once you get a decent number of pins—say 30 or 40—look through them and see if there are certain styles that appear over and over. If so, that's the style you gravitate toward and probably what you want to order for your wedding.

Square Tiers vs. Round Tiers

When it comes to cakes, the first thing you need to know is the difference between a layer and a tier. When you bake a cake at home, it generally has two layers, separated by frosting. This is a one-tier cake. When you see a traditional wedding cake with a small, medium, and large tier stacked on top of each other, that's a three-tier cake. Each tier probably has three or more layers within it.

Your bakery will help you figure out how many tiers your cake needs to be to serve the number of guests expected at your wedding. But you need to figure out whether you want those tiers to be square, round, or something else. You could do heart-shaped tiers, triangles, hexagons—really, any geometric shape. Round is the most traditional; square is a little edgier (no pun intended).

Buttercream vs. Fondant

When it comes to frosting, there are basically two types: buttercream and fondant. Buttercream is exactly what it sounds like—it's primarily made of butter. It's very light, airy, and fluffy. It's easy to slice through and eat, but it is temperature-sensitive and can melt in the sun. If you're having a fully outdoor summer wedding, buttercream may not be the way to go.

Fondant is actually icing that's been rolled very thin and is then draped over the cake tier and pressed into place. It creates an ultra-smooth surface with clean lines. It's also sometimes called "rolled fondant" because it's rolled out. It holds up better in the heat, but can be difficult to cut into and eat because it's much thicker than buttercream frosting.

Or maybe you'll end up loving the look of "naked" cakes that have just a grazing of buttercream frosting. This is why you need Pinterest. You don't know what you like until you see it.

Fresh Flowers vs. Sugar ("Gum Paste") Flowers

If you plan to decorate your cake with flowers, you can do fresh or sugar. Fresh flowers work better with a buttercream frosting, while sugar or gum paste flowers are ideal for either buttercream or fondant. Not all fresh flowers are suitable for cake decorating because some are toxic. Be sure to discuss with your florist which flowers are safe to use (and you'll want them to be pesticide-free).

Fresh flowers work well with buttercream because the frosting is soft, and you can press the flower stems into the frosting to keep them in place. Fondant creates a hard surface unsuitable for pressing flowers into. Instead, the sugar flowers are "glued" to the fondant using a dab of icing. You can also use sugar flowers on a buttercream-frosted cake.

Keep in mind that sugar flowers are expensive due to the amount of experience, skill, and labor required to produce them. If budget is a concern, fresh flowers will be a better choice.

Color Scheme

Don't forget to consider your overall wedding color scheme and think about how you want to incorporate it into your wedding cake. Maybe you want an all-white cake with flowers to match your color scheme. Or maybe you want the frosting to match your color scheme with a neutral cake topper and no flowers. Again, look at what you gravitated toward on Pinterest to help you narrow your choices.

Bonus tip: when shopping for cake toppers, Etsy is a gold mine. You can find anything you want on Etsy, including custom options.

Limit your tasting options

The bakery will ask you to select a few different batter and filling combinations to taste during your appointment. This isn't because they're trying to short-change you. It's because they offer so many options, there's no way you could make a decision faced with that number of flavors. Limiting yourself to 4-6 flavors will enable you to actually make a decision.

I generally recommend that each tier of your cake be a different flavor, so you can offer your guests a few different options. Not everyone likes chocolate cake. (Shocking, I know!)

If you or your guests have allergies, discuss those with your bakery to see what they offer. You would be surprised at how good a gluten-, dairy-, and egg-free cake can taste. If that's something you want to consider, be sure to ask to taste it at your appointment.

The anniversary tier

It's a traditional wedding custom to save the top tier of your wedding cake, stick it in the freezer for a year, and eat it on your first wedding anniversary. This is a terrible idea. Cake is not designed to be frozen for a year. There's no way it will taste anywhere near as good as it did on your wedding day.

Some bakeries offer a free anniversary cake when you spend a certain minimum amount on your wedding cake. This is vastly superior to saving part of your actual wedding cake. Even if your bakery doesn't have a similar program, you can always order a small cake from them for your anniversary. I assure you it will taste much better than if you had saved the top tier.

Money-saving tip

If your budget is tight, there's a simple way to cut down on cake costs. Instead of ordering a four-tier, fancy decorated cake to serve 150 people, order a small, one-tier, fancy decorated cake just for display and cutting. Then ask the bakery to make sheet cakes in the flavor combinations you liked best. The sheet cakes can be stashed in the kitchen, then sliced, plated, and served by the catering staff. No one will be the wiser. (Plus, it's actually a lot easier to slice sheet cakes than a large multi-tier cake anyway.)

Non-Cake Wedding Desserts

A towering wedding cake can be a show-stopper at your wedding reception. But what if you aren't a cake lover? Do you still have to have a wedding cake? The answer is no!

Your wedding dessert options are limited only by your imagination. As I always tell my clients when they ask me if they "have" to do something: it's your wedding. It should be a reflection of your and your partner's personalities. If you don't love cake, you don't have to serve cake.

But what if you have a relative (read: mom) who insists that you can't have a wedding without a wedding cake? It's probably because she wants the photos of the cake cutting. In that case, why not compromise? Have the dessert you want, but have a small, single-tier cake just for cutting. It doesn't need to be sliced and served to guests, but you have it for the cake cutting photo op. Win-win. Most bakeries offer small cakes designed for this very purpose.

Here are some other ideas for non-cake wedding desserts.

Cupcakes

Cupcakes are sort of the OG of alternative wedding desserts. They're nice because nothing needs to be sliced and plated, and they are self-serve. Plus, it's easy to have many different flavors of cupcake. With a wedding cake, each tier can be a different flavor, but if you only have two tiers, you're limited to two flavors.

But beware: don't decide on cupcakes because you think it will save you money. It takes a lot of time and effort to frost all those individual cupcakes. They can easily cost just as much as (or more than) a wedding cake.

Cake pops

It started with baby showers and has made its way to weddings — the cake pop phenomenon is still going strong. As with cupcakes, cake pops make a great dessert because there's no large cake to slice, and guests can grab their own cake pop. Bonus: they're easily transportable (when they're wrapped in cellophane) so guests can take one for the road.

Doughnuts (or donuts, if you insist)

There are a few ways to serve doughnuts. Doughnut display walls with pegs have become popular in the past couple years. But make sure your doughnuts aren't too gooey, or this doesn't work at all because they slide off the pegs.

I once had a client assemble a "cake" out of Krispy Kremes. We used a tiered stand and arranged the doughnuts on top of each other on each tier to make it appear that it was a cake. We even put a topper on it. Doughnuts can also be stacked on trays on a buffet table.

Pie

With pie you can have large pies to be cut and served as slices, or you can do smaller, personal pies for each guest. Again, the smaller the unit, the more versatility you have with choosing flavors. And you can do a variety of fruit pies alongside something like a Boston Cream for variety.

Ice cream

Sundae bar, anyone? Imagine all the sundae fixings lined up on the buffet. Your guests choose their favorite ice cream flavor from a (limited) selection, it's served to them in a compote cup, and then they get to customize with sprinkles and nuts and drizzles to their heart's content.

Cookies

In some cultures, it's common for the family members of the couple to bake cookies and bring them to the wedding for a cookie buffet. But even if that's not one of your cultural traditions, you can still order cookies from a bakery and have a cookie buffet.

Or do a buffet with cookies, brownies, Rice Krispy treats and other childhood favorites. French macarons make for a colorful display and have the added bonus of being light and airy, so no one feels weighed down by dessert.

Hot chocolate station

Perfect for a smaller fall or winter wedding. You can offer a buffet with options to dress your hot chocolate—whipped cream, caramel, nutmeg, cinnamon, whiskey, rum…the list goes on.

Culturally traditional desserts

A croquembouche is a traditional French dessert, which is essentially a cake, but not what we Americans generally think of when it comes to wedding cake.

Some Pakistani clients of mine served a buffet of traditional Pakistani desserts in lieu of cake because most of their guests weren't cake lovers. If you have a culturally specific dessert that you would like to serve at your wedding, it's a great way to add another personal touch to your day.

Chocolate fountain

Chocolate fountains used to be really popular, but they've waned a bit in the past decade, plus they have a bit of a "Las Vegas convention" feel to them. But there are so many goodies that can be dipped in a chocolate fountain: pretzels, Rice Krispy treats, vanilla wafer cookies, marshmallows, berries, graham crackers. Plus, they make a fun photo op.

S'mores

Speaking of graham crackers—s'mores! This idea really only works if your wedding reception is taking place outside and you have access to one or more fire pits, but many outdoor venues are making this part of their wedding packages. You can go the traditional route with Nabisco Honey Grahams, Kraft Marshmallows, and Hershey bars, or you can make it artisanal with homemade graham crackers, homemade vanilla marshmallows, and dark chocolate. You'll just want to make sure you have plenty of fire-safe skewers available.

Mix and Match

The greatest thing about the above options is that you can combine some of them. Do a buffet of cupcakes, doughnuts, and cookies. Have cake AND cake pops! Offer s'mores WITH a hot chocolate bar. So. Many. Desserts.

Your Homework Assignment

I'll give you one guess what I'm going to say! Get recommendations from friends, browse Instagram, check the preferred lists of your venue and coordinator, then move on to looking at different bakeries' websites. Most bakeries and pastry specialists these days have websites, but you will occasionally find one who doesn't. Unlike with photographers, I don't let the lack of a website deter me when investigating bakeries. You should definitely ask them to send you a gallery or portfolio of images from weddings they've done in the past.

Use the Bakery Questionnaire to help you ask the right questions. Find the Bakery Questionnaire at www.risajamesevents.com/wedding-questionnaires. Schedule one to three tasting appointments and then choose your favorite.

Hair and Makeup

Brides will likely have professional hair and makeup services for their wedding day. Here are the things you need to know when scheduling wedding hair and makeup.

First, decide how many people will be having hair and makeup services. Generally, it's the bride, her female attendants (maid of honor and bridesmaids), the mother of the bride, the mother of the groom, any step-mothers, and potentially close family members who aren't part of the wedding party.

The number one rule of wedding hair and makeup is that if you, as the bride, are *requiring* someone to have professional hair and makeup services, you should pay for those services. It's rude to demand that a bridesmaid spend $100-300 on hair and makeup.

If you don't want to pay for everyone's hair and makeup, then make those services optional. That way the ones who want to and can afford it will have professional services, and the ones who don't or can't will do their own hair and makeup.

Some wedding beauty professionals provide both hair and makeup services and some do one or the other. Once you know how many people need services, you can determine how many stylists you need.

On average, it will take an hour for each of the bride's services — that is, an hour for hair and another hour for makeup — and 45–60 minutes per service per person for anyone else.

If you have 8 people having hair and makeup (bride, mother of the bride, mother of the groom, maid of honor, 4 bridesmaids), that's at least 14 hours of services. You need a team of beauty professionals to pull that off.

Even if you hire one hairstylist and one makeup artist, that still going to require 7 hours of your day for hair and makeup. Two hairstylists and two makeup artists can provide hair and makeup services for 8 people in under four hours, which is far more manageable.

In a case where there are two brides, I recommend hiring two separate teams of beauty professionals so each bride can have her own space with her own team. This is especially true if each bride has several female attendants.

If only the brides are having professional hair and makeup, then they could share a hairstylist and makeup artist. One bride would have hair while the other was in makeup, and then the professionals would switch brides.

Things to keep in mind:

1. Each stylist will need about 15 minutes to unpack and set up their equipment, so if they arrive at 10 am, the first appointment will be at 10:15.

2. Many beauty professionals only accept cash (or maybe Venmo) on the wedding day, so make sure you know what the total will be and bring enough cash.

3. If the beauty professionals work for a company, salon, or agency, plan to tip 15-20% of the total. For beauty pros who own their own business and set their own rates, tipping is optional.

4. Ask any questions you have during the booking process: do they use vegan or cruelty-free products? Do they airbrush makeup or use hair extensions? Will they place your veil or other hair décor?

5. If you have a floral hair decoration, make sure it's delivered by your florist before the hairstylist departs so they can place it and make sure it's secure. If you're not getting ready at the same venue where the wedding is being held, you may need to pay extra for your florist to make a second delivery.

6. Have water and snacks on hand during the getting ready session, and offer them to your hairstylist and makeup artist. They'll probably bring their own, but it's still nice to offer.

7. Schedule a trial-run with both the hairstylist and the makeup artist before you pay your deposit and book with them. You want to make sure you like their work. Bring inspiration photos so they have some idea of the look you want.

8. Choose your venue wisely. We covered this in the Venue section, but it's worth repeating. If your wedding venue has a getting ready space, make sure you look at it during your tour. Does it have lots of windows and natural light? What about mirrors? What's the seating situation? Stools, armless chairs, or salon chairs are ideal. Both your stylists and your photographer will love you if there's a lot of good, natural light in the room.

Follow these tips, and your wedding hair and makeup will be a success.

Your Homework Assignment

Decide whether you want to pay for hair and makeup for all your bridesmaids. If you have a regular stylist, ask if they do weddings (not all of them do). Ask friends or your wedding coordinator for recommendations. Reach out to those pros for more information, such as pricing, whether they come to you or you have to go to them, and portfolios. Use the Hair & Makeup Questionnaire to help you ask the right questions. Find the Hair & Makeup Questionnaire at www.risajamesevents.com/wedding-questionnaires.

Schedule a trial with your top choice (maybe on the day of your engagement photos) and have some idea of what you want to do with your hair and makeup. After the trial, decide whether you want to lock in that pro for your wedding day or try someone else. (Note: in-demand hair and makeup pros will not have as much scheduling flexibility, and you may need to sign a contract and pay a deposit before scheduling a trial.)

Officiant

There are three non-negotiable requirements to have a marriage ceremony: consent by both parties, a valid license, and someone to solemnize the marriage. The person who has the authority to solemnize the marriage is your wedding officiant. So how do you choose a wedding officiant?

Who can officiate a wedding?

There are essentially four categories of people who can legally officiate a wedding:

1. ordained clergy who belong to a religious organization;
2. a federal or state official, such as a judge or justice of the peace;
3. a professional wedding officiant not affiliated with a house of worship or employed by a government entity; or
4. a friend or family member.

The first three categories of officiant can perform marriages in any state, but there may be limitations on whether a friend or family member can be ordained online and then legally perform your wedding ceremony. So be sure to check your state laws before deciding on this route. Ask your wedding planner/coordinator, or Google it.

Ordained Clergy

Ordained clergy are priests, rabbis, ministers — people who are affiliated with a religious sect and lead a congregation regularly in worship at a house of worship. Depending on the religion, clergy may be willing to perform your ceremony somewhere other than in the house of worship (church, synagogue, mosque, etc.) or they may require your ceremony to take place in the official house of worship.

The Catholic Church, in particular, frowns upon marriage ceremonies held outside of an actual Catholic church. I have had Catholic clients who had two wedding ceremonies: the sacramental one at their church led by their priest, and then a separate one led by someone else at an off-site location.

Muslim and Jewish weddings are not generally required to be held in a house of worship, but only you know for sure the limitations and restrictions of your religion. Speak with your clergy person if you have questions or concerns.

Very few of my clients have ceremonies in houses of worship these days. It's much more common to hold the ceremony and reception in the same location, regardless of who's performing the ceremony.

Government Officials

If you are eloping at the city or county courthouse, you're more likely to have a judge or justice of the peace presiding at your wedding ceremony. They are authorized by law to solemnize marriages. (The solemnization is the part where the officiant says, "By the power vested in me by the State of [insert state name] I now pronounce you [insert "married" or "husband and wife" or "wife and wife" etc.].)

But eloping in the courthouse isn't the only way to have a judge or justice of the peace as your officiant. If you know a judge, feel free to ask them if they would be willing to officiate your wedding.

Friend or Family Member

This has become the most common choice for many couples getting married today. What's great about it is that you can choose someone who's very close to you to be a special part of your wedding day. One of my brothers officiated my wedding, and then I officiated his a few years later.

However, check your state laws. Not all states will allow just anyone to become ordained and officiate a wedding. Some states allow it only "temporarily" for one wedding; others allow anyone ordained at any time in the past to conduct weddings. Some states don't allow it at all.

Getting ordained is super easy. The two sites I recommend to my clients are Universal Life Church and American Marriage Ministries. Ordination is free and fast. Some organizations will tell you that you need to order a certificate or other paraphernalia. You probably don't. In many states, no "proof of ordination" is required. The officiant signs the marriage license in the appropriate place, enters "minister" as their occupation, and lists the name of the entity that ordained them. That's it. No certification number, no certificate necessary. So check your local state laws and regulations if you have questions.

Professional Wedding Officiant

Professional wedding officiants are non-denominational and can perform religious or secular wedding ceremonies. They will work with you to craft a ceremony that represents you as a couple and your shared values. While many couples today opt to have a friend or family member perform the ceremony, there are many advantages to hiring a professional officiant.

The Pros of Hiring a Pro

1. Pros know how to deal with mishaps, such as the sound cutting out or a microphone failing mid-ceremony. They won't get flustered when things go awry.

2. They are trained public speakers. They know how to enunciate and project so that everyone can hear them.

3. There's no chance they'll get stage fright and cancel on you at the last minute.

4. They know how to properly sign the marriage license. States are VERY particular when it comes to official documents like marriage licenses. Any mistakes and you have to go back to the county clerk and get a new license and start all over again.

5. They can make your ceremony as personal as you want it to be. They have experience with lots of wedding ceremonies and can craft something that's uniquely "you."

What to Ask a Prospective Officiant

1. Do they have any sample ceremonies that you can build from and customize for your own ceremony? Every ceremony is different, but most of them include standard elements. It can help if you're not starting from scratch.

2. Will they help you design special elements and vows? This could be anything from a secret question posed to both halves of the couple to a live butterfly release.

3. Will they take care of mailing the paperwork after the ceremony? This is especially important if you're leaving for your honeymoon immediately after the wedding. Can you trust someone in your family to get your marriage license mailed in? Better to leave it to a responsible professional.

4. Do they have reviews from past clients that you can read?

5. What is their fee, and what's included? Is there a travel fee or an additional fee for the rehearsal?

6. And one final question that's really for you: are you comfortable with this person? Your marriage ceremony is the most intimate portion of your wedding day. You want to be sure you connect with your officiant on a personal level. I recommend meeting with them, if possible. If not, then at least a phone call is required.

Your Homework Assignment

Start by discussing who you think you want to officiate your marriage. If you both agree, ask that person if they are willing to perform the honor. If you want to hire a professional officiant, solicit recommendations from your friends or other wedding pros and start researching and scheduling consultations until you find the right fit.

Use the Officiant Questionnaire to help you ask the right questions. Find the Officiant Questionnaire at www.risajamesevents.com/wedding-questionnaires.

CHAPTER 5

The Details

Do You Need a Wedding Website?

The short answer is YES! Whenever I'm asked this question, I encourage my clients to go ahead and set up a wedding website. It's not hard to do, and it's a useful repository of information for your guests. Being able to find all the relevant wedding information in one, easy-to-access place is so convenient.

What goes on the site?

- **Information about the wedding**: time and location of ceremony and reception, addresses, and special notes. Maybe your ceremony will be on the lawn and you want to warn guests to wear wedge heels rather than stilettos. Perhaps the air conditioning will be blasting all night and guests will want to bring a wrap or a sweater. Anything they need to know can go in this section.

- **Travel information**: airport and car rental availability, descriptions and links to hotels near the wedding location (whether or not you've set up room blocks—more on this later), an embedded map link so guests can easily see the surrounding area.

- **Things to do**: what would you recommend to out-of-towners? Are there wineries or breweries to visit? A local zoo or aquarium? Kid-friendly activities? Your guests are coming for the wedding, but there's a lot of time in a weekend that won't be spent at the wedding, so help them find something to do. A list of your favorite restaurants and coffee shops will be appreciated.

- **Photos and write-up of the couple**: how did you meet, what was the proposal like, what are your plans post-wedding? This is a great way to show off your engagement photos!

- **Photos and write-up of the wedding party members**: how do you know them, why are they special to you, what do you want people to know about them? You can even include photos of you and/or your fiancé(e) with each person, if you have them.

- **RSVP option**: a time-saver for you and your guests! No more waiting for the post office to deliver mailed response cards. You also won't have to enter RSVP and meal selection information into your spreadsheet if your website is already keeping track of it. Some tech-forward couples are doing away with the paper response card altogether and only having online RSVPs. This saves money (as well as trees) because you don't have to pay for the response cards and envelopes, or for postage. (Note: you're supposed to pre-stamp the return envelope for the response card.)

- **Registry information and links**: this might be the single most useful feature of a wedding website. If you've registered at two or three stores, your guests will have to go to the website for each store, find their "Registry" link, input one of your names, then select the correct registry information. You save everyone a lot of hassle by putting the information right there on your website with a link that will take guests directly to your registry.

Where can you create a wedding website?

Lots of places! The Knot and WeddingWire both offer free wedding websites as part of their service. Zola is another option, both for registering for gifts and for creating a wedding website. If you order your invitations from Minted, they have website templates to match most of their invitation designs. They offer a free version, but if you want a custom URL (without minted.us as part of it) the fee is minimal. Appy Couple offers both websites and an optional phone app to make it even easier for your guests to keep tabs on your wedding information. As with Minted, you can pay a small fee to have a custom URL, and they offer invitations.

You can also use a more traditional website builder platform like Squarespace or Wix. These sites aren't free, but you will get far more features and functionality with them. And you don't need to know how to write code to use them.

Lastly, consider Wordpress.com if you're interested in doing a more blog-style website. This is the approach I took when I got married. Most of my family and friends lived far away from me, and I wanted them to be able to share in the wedding planning process with me. So I wrote posts with photos at each milestone along the way — venue shopping, dress shopping, cake tasting, registering, etc. It was a fun way to keep everyone in the loop. Plus, we also had all that information mentioned above on there.

How do you let people know about your wedding website?

The best way is to put it on your save-the-date card/magnet/email—whatever format you're using to get the word out that you are getting married. Save-the-dates are typically sent 6–9 months before the wedding, so your website may not be complete at that point, but guests can follow along as you add more information throughout the planning process.

If you're not sending save-the-dates, you can include an insert with your invitation providing the URL for your wedding website. I don't recommend putting the website URL on the invitation itself, because you want to keep the invitation elegant, and website URLs are the opposite of elegant. But a matching insert card is a classy way of conveying the information.

On the other hand, if you're having a bridal shower, those invitations are the perfect place to list your wedding website. Guests will want to know where you're registered, and they'll know that the website is where they can find that information.

And if none of those options works for you, then there's always good old email or word of mouth to let people know about the site.

Don't feel discouraged by the prospect of setting up a wedding website if you're not a "techie." Most of these platforms have made it as simple as possible for you to create a site.

A Note About Address Collection

Some wedding website companies give you the option to add guest addresses (along with email addresses) right in their platform. If you order your wedding invitations from the same company that hosts your website, they will have a specific format in which you need to upload your guest list. Every website is different, so it can be helpful for you to determine where you want to host your website and order your invitations before you begin collecting addresses.

Your Homework Assignment

Start thinking now about how and where you want to host your wedding website. Once you've chosen your invitation suite (more on that later), investigate whether your invitation provider also provides wedding websites. Get your website URL established before you send save-the-dates, even if you haven't put anything on your wedding website yet.

Wedding Don'ts

Have you ever been to a wedding and thought, "I would never do that at my wedding"? I have, and I'm always left wondering how on earth the couple could have made such a blunder. One of my roles as a wedding planner is to offer advice to my clients (and friends). But if they don't ask, then I don't have the opportunity to weigh in. So here's my unsolicited advice about five things you absolutely should not do at your wedding.

1. Cash Bar

I know I mentioned this previously, but it's worth repeating. Never, ever charge your guests. When you throw a party, you are acting as host and offering your guests your hospitality. Charging them turns it into a business transaction. If you can't afford to offer a full open bar for multiple hours for potentially hundreds of people, don't. There are many alternatives you can consider.

Serve only beer and wine. Serve liquor for a limited time (such as only at cocktail hour) and then switch to beer and wine for the rest of the reception. Serve only two signature cocktails instead of a full bar, which drastically cuts down on the amount of alcohol the bar needs to have on hand. Offer a fun non-alcoholic option, like a juice bar.

In short, do anything other than a cash bar.

2. Schedule Gaps

In keeping with the theme of hospitality, it is rude to your guests to have a long break between the end of your ceremony and the beginning of your reception, unless you are providing an activity for them during that in-between time. Sometimes a long gap between ceremony and reception occurs because the couple want to take photos during that time but not miss cocktail hour.

This is why first-look sessions became popular. You get the vast majority of your photos out of the way before the ceremony, allowing you to transition smoothly from ceremony to reception without missing the action.

If you just can't face the idea of seeing your partner before the ceremony, then you'll have to miss cocktail hour to get those photos. Sorry. If you want to be a good host, those are your options.

3. Starting Late

You've invited your nearest and dearest to witness your marriage vows. These people have planned their day (possibly their weekend) around your wedding. They have perhaps traveled and foregone other activities and events. They spent time getting ready and arrived on time. Show them the courtesy of beginning on time.

A five-minute delay is perfectly acceptable and gives everyone time to get settled in their seats. A 30-minute delay is unconscionable. If you are a person who is habitually late for everything, assign one of your attendants to be your time-minder for the day.

Your wedding planner will do her best to keep you on schedule, but if the bride or groom arrives at the venue 30 minutes late, there's nothing anyone can do to get things back on track. So don't be late!

4. Registry Information on the Invitation

Your registry information should never appear on a wedding invitation. Everyone knows that when you're invited to a wedding, you should send a gift to the couple. And the registry makes that process significantly easier. But it's improper to include the registry on the invitation because it gives the appearance of demanding (or at the very least, soliciting) a gift.

Before the rise of the Internet and the prevalence of save-the-date announcements, registry information was primarily shared via word-of-mouth. These days, it's much more common for the couple to create a wedding website, include a page with links to their registries (2–3 at most), and include the wedding website URL on the save-the-date card. As I mentioned in the previous section about wedding websites, if you're not sending save-the-dates, you can include an insert card with your invitation that lists your wedding website URL, but don't put the URL directly on the invitation.

The only invitation on which registry information should appear is a bridal shower invite. Because the purpose of the bridal shower is to "shower" the bride with gifts, it is reasonable (and practically necessary) to include the registry information.

5. Children & Animals in Your Wedding Party

There's an old Hollywood adage that you should never work with children or animals, because they are unpredictable and uncontrollable. The same holds true for weddings.

If you are a laid-back, chill person, then by all means, include children and animals in your wedding. But if you're the kind of person who gets upset when the slightest thing goes wrong, you should consider only adult humans as part of your big day. Don't get me wrong, small children and animals (usually dogs) can be totally adorable. You just have to be prepared for, and comfortable with, the unexpected.

A short list of things I've seen at weddings: a young flower girl vomited mid-ceremony; a dog burrowed under the bride's dress; one flower girl chastised the other (her little sister) for not properly tossing the petals; a ring bearer stopped halfway down the aisle and refused to walk any further; a ring bearer threw a tantrum moments before the ceremony and had to be removed; a canine ring bearer barked throughout the ceremony.

I've never seen anyone try to incorporate a cat into a wedding ceremony, but given the general uncooperativeness of cats, I imagine it would be a disaster. Older children do better than young children for obvious reasons. The take-away here is that you should carefully think through whether the children or pets in question are capable of performing on cue. If not, it might be best to leave them out.

Your Homework Assignment

Easy: don't do any of the above. Except maybe involve children or animals in your wedding if you're okay with things potentially going wrong.

Bride's Attire

The hunt for The Dress can be a lot of things: fun, exhilarating, exciting, exhausting, frustrating. Many girls' first wedding dress experience comes when they try on their mother's gown as a child. They picture their own wedding day and fantasize about feeling and looking like a princess. (Or not. If you never played dress-up or imagined what your wedding dress would look like, you're in good company.)

Here are the tips I give brides-to-be when they begin searching for what is likely to be the most expensive item of clothing they ever purchase.

Start early

You almost can't start dress-shopping too soon. That said, you shouldn't start dress-shopping until you have an idea of the overall style and formality of your event. You don't want your dress to look out-of-place in your venue. So wait until you have your venue booked and you've decided on a time of day for your wedding before you begin shopping for your gown.

There are generally three ways to buy a wedding gown: off-the-rack, made-to-order, and custom-made (a.k.a. couture). Unless you are willing to spend tens of thousands of dollars, you are probably not going to have a custom-made gown. That approach is generally taken by celebrities and wealthy individuals. A designer/tailor cuts fabric to your exact measurements and sews it just for you. A custom gown is also one-of-a-kind.

Most bridal salons operate on a made-to-order (also known as "made-to-measure") basis. They have in the store one "sample" size of each dress they carry. You will try on that sample dress, and the stylist will use clips to cinch it into place so you can get a better idea of what it would look like if it were properly fitted. Once you choose a dress, the stylist takes a variety of measurements of your body, and then decides which size dress you should order. The dress won't fit you perfectly when it arrives, but the goal is to get close enough that minor alterations will make it perfect. (Keep in mind that bridal gown sizing bears no relation to either reality or regular dress sizing. If you normally wear a size 4 dress, it is not at all unusual for you to need a size 10 wedding dress.)

Off-the-rack is just what it sounds like. You try on a dress in the store, and you walk out with that exact dress. This is how David's Bridal and bridal outlets operate, as well as sample sales held by salons. David's Bridal keeps multiple sizes of every gown in stock. You try on and buy the size that fits you best. At sample sales, you're buying the salon's sample dress that has been tried on by potentially hundreds of women. You can save a lot of money on the dress itself, but alterations and cleaning will set you back.

If you're not buying off-the-rack, you will have to wait several months after placing your order for your dress to arrive. Gown manufacturers do not cut and sew dresses as each order comes in. They wait until they have a number of orders for a given size, and then they cut them all at once. This is why you should start your dress search at least six months before your wedding, if possible. Once the dress arrives, you also have to allow several weeks for alterations.

Do some research

It doesn't matter which bridal magazine or website you choose to do your research—*Martha Stewart Weddings, Bride's, Grace Ormond Wedding Style, The Knot*—they will all showcase a multitude of dresses, and often feature articles on how to choose the best dress for your body type. Try to ignore the wafer-thin models contorted into ridiculous poses and picture how the dress will look on YOU. If you're reading a magazine, tear out pages of dresses you like so you can take them with you when you go dress shopping. If you're browsing online, start a Pinterest board for dresses. Then you can pull up the app on your phone while shopping and give your bridal salon stylist some idea of what you like. Even after you've found styles you like, be sure to keep an open mind. If a bridal stylist thinks a certain type of dress would look good on you, but you hadn't previously considered that style, go ahead and try it on. You might be surprised!

Choose three local bridal salons and make appointments

I recommend visiting no more than three shops because you will become overwhelmed with options otherwise. Studies show that humans have optimal decision-making skills when their choices are limited.

It's important to have an appointment so that you know someone will be available to help you locate dresses and try them on. It can be very difficult to find a dress at a salon when they are all on hangers and crammed onto racks. If you tell your stylist you want a ball gown with a tulle skirt, she will know where in the store to find those dresses. Having a stylist to help you is essential when trying on gowns. Most bridal salons require appointments, but even if they don't require it, appointments are recommended.

Don't schedule all your appointments on the same day if you can avoid it

Trying on wedding gowns is a surprising amount of work. The gowns are heavy and difficult to get into. If the weather is warm when you're trying them on, you will quickly become overwhelmed.

Take someone with you, but no more than two people

The most obvious choices for a second opinion are your mother and your maid of honor. Lately, more brides are actually dress-shopping with their partners. I, personally, don't recommend this approach, because the moment when your future spouse sees you for the first time in your wedding dress should be on your wedding day, when excitement levels are high and your hair and makeup look perfect. Not in a bridal salon with fluorescent lighting when you're likely to be cranky from getting into and out of heavy gowns over and over again.

There are two reasons why I recommend taking no more than two people with you. First, many bridal salons do not have the space to accommodate a large entourage, and some even place limits on how many guests can accompany you. Second, there is such a thing as too many opinions. If you have too many people with you, you are unlikely to ever find a dress that everyone thinks is perfect for you. That said, take at least one objective person with you. Bridal salon stylists will be honest with you up to a point, but let's face it, they want to make a sale. And no one will be more honest with you than your mother or your best friend. (Okay, your mother might be a little *too* honest.)

Set a dress budget ahead of time and don't try on anything that is way above your budget

Weddings can be very expensive, and your wedding dress will almost certainly be the most expensive garment you ever buy. It's important to have a budget in mind BEFORE you start shopping, and stick to it. If your budget is $1000, and you try on a dress that's $1200, that's okay. If you decide you simply must have that gown, you'll be able to offset the extra $200 elsewhere in your overall wedding budget. But don't try on a dress that's $3000. You might fall in love with it, and then you'll either be heartbroken that you can't afford it, or you'll blow your budget and have to completely re-imagine your entire wedding. There is a bountiful selection of bridal gowns in the $1500-or-less category. Yes, there are gowns that cost $10,000 or more. Yes, they are stunning. But you can find a stunning gown no matter what your price point is.

Also, when setting your budget, don't forget that the cost of the dress is not the only factor in the overall "attire" category. You will need shoes, possibly undergarments, alterations, and accessories. The dress is certainly the largest portion of your "attire" budget line item, but you should pad the total budgeted amount to accommodate the extras. (And don't forget that your partner's attire goes in the same budget category.)

Wear appropriate undergarments and bring shoes

Even if you don't plan to try on strapless gowns, it's wise to wear a strapless or long-line bra when you visit bridal salons. That way you won't have to worry about straps interfering with how the gown really looks on you. Also, modesty kind of goes out the window when trying on a dress that requires assistance to get into and out of. Skip the thong and wear full-coverage underwear. Lastly, bring heels that are approximately the same height as you want to wear on your wedding day. This is essential when you're having your dress fittings, but is also a good idea when dress-shopping.

Have someone take a photo of you wearing the dresses you like best, but ask the stylist's permission first

Trying on wedding gowns is like apartment-hunting—everything starts to blend together in your mind after looking at just a couple. Having photos of what the dresses look like on you is the best way to remember details and compare later. Even if you think you've found The One, I recommend taking a night to "sleep on it" to be certain. Going back to photos can be helpful. Most bridal salons allow photography, but a few don't, and it's always polite to ask.

Don't be disappointed if you don't break down and cry when you find your dress

Bridal magazines and television shows like *Say Yes to the Dress* do prospective brides a disservice by pushing a false narrative about dress-shopping. Yes, it's a more special shopping occasion than most, but it's not a magical experience full of fairy dust and unicorns. The gown isn't what makes your wedding day memorable. Choose the gown that (1) you are comfortable in, (2) flatters you, (3) fits within your budget, and (4) your fiancé(e) will like.

Don't let yourself be talked into unnecessary extras or in-store alterations

If you've decided you don't want to wear a veil, don't let someone talk you into buying a veil. You can wear a fascinator, or a tiara, or a birdcage veil, or flowers, or jeweled clips, or nothing at all in your hair. And if you do want to wear a veil, you don't have to buy it at the same place you buy your dress. As for for slips, underskirts, and tulle layers, don't purchase anything until you have a chance to try it on with your gown. Even if the designer or the stylist recommends a particular underskirt, you may find that you like the dress better without it.

As for alterations, bridal salons have an in-house alterations department, but that doesn't mean you have to use it. You are free to take your gown to anyone you want for alterations (and don't let the salon tell you otherwise). In fact, if you want to make significant alterations — not just sizing, but style, such as adding or removing sleeves — you may have to go elsewhere. Some salons are bound by contracts with the designers as to the extent of alterations they are allowed to make. Those contracts are not binding on you, as the purchaser, or on any other third party. This is something to keep in mind if an in-house seamstress tells you she "can't" do something you want.

Bonus tip: Don't forget to have fun!

Shopping for your wedding gown is a once-in-a-lifetime event. Have fun with it and enjoy yourself. Try to schedule your appointments on a day when you can take your time, and maybe even schedule a fun lunch (with Champagne!) for yourself and your companion(s). Don't get discouraged if you've tried on several dresses and still haven't found one you love. The right dress is out there.

Your Homework Assignment

Start looking at gowns online or in magazines and get a feel for what styles you like. Keep in mind your venue and the time of year you're getting married, as well as your body type. Certain styles of gowns look better on certain body types, and all the models in the magazines are thin, tall, and willowy, so they're not super helpful.

Research bridal salons in your area (Google is always your best friend for this) and schedule one appointment to start. If you don't find anything you love at the first appointment, schedule another one. Repeat until you've purchased your dress, then purchase a veil or any other accessories you may want.

Groom's Attire

When it comes to weddings, the bride's dress gets all the attention, but wedding attire for the groom is important too. This also applies to brides who want to wear a suit instead of a gown. Here's what you need to know about groom style.

Tuxedo or Suit?

When it comes to pants-based wedding attire, you have three basic options: tuxedo, suit, or something more casual. A tuxedo is your most formal option and is best for indoor weddings and those taking place in the evening. Traditionally, tuxedos were only appropriate for ceremonies being held at 6 p.m. or later, but that "rule" is bent more often than not these days.

Tuxedos also come in a much wider variety than they used to—especially tuxedos for women. You can find striking black and white tuxes, but also stunning burgundy, blue, and grey. No matter what style you want, you can probably find it.

A suit is suitable (no pun intended) for both indoor and outdoor ceremonies and any time of day. If your wedding is taking place in the morning or early afternoon, you probably want to go with a lighter color—blue or grey. Late afternoon or evening weddings can handle darker colors like navy, charcoal, and burgundy. The season matters too. Dark colors are more appropriate in fall and winter, whereas lighter colors work better in spring and summer.

But if a suit or tuxedo is not your jam, then you still have other options. A light-colored pair of trousers with a navy blazer is a classic "New England country club" look. Or maybe you want to do trousers with vests or suspenders, but no jacket. This is a great alternative for really hot summer months. If you're getting married on a beach, consider linen pants and shirts.

Ties & Vests

For neckwear, you have two main options: long necktie or bow tie. It used to be that bow ties were always worn with tuxedos, but long ties are becoming more common with a formal look. You can get custom ties in any color, pattern, or print that you want. Etsy is full of shops offering custom neckwear.

Vests are another way to bring color to the outfit. They can be worn with or without a jacket. Generally speaking, the vest and tie should match each other. They should either be the same color or the same pattern.

When selecting ties and vests, this is a good opportunity to set the groom apart from the groomsmen. Even if everyone is wearing the same color tux or suit, the groom should have a different color tie and vest than the groomsmen. It indicates that he's special.

When there are two grooms in the wedding, they can either match each other, while having the wedding party wear a different color. Or each groom can do something different with his accessories.

One thing to keep in mind with two grooms is that if they are both dressed in the same color tux or suit, they can blend into each other in photos. If you think about a bride wearing white and a groom wearing black, they create contrast in photos.

But with two grooms wearing black, it's hard to see where one ends and the other begins when they are embracing or otherwise standing very close to one another in photos. So you might consider dressing one groom in a lighter color and the other in a darker color — but still complementary to one another.

Cufflinks & Pocket Squares

Two other relevant accessories are cuff links and pocket squares. Cuff links are always worn with tuxedos but are optional with suits or jacket/trouser combos.

Button-down dress shirts come in two different cuff types: barrel and French. A French cuff shirt is more formal than a barrel cuff. The barrel cuff is probably what you picture when you think of a button-down shirt. The sleeve has buttons on it, and the sleeve closes by overlapping one edge over the other.

A French cuff sleeve doesn't overlap — rather, the two ends pinch together to form a bit of a peak that juts out from the sleeve, and they are held together by cufflinks or silk knots.

Pocket squares are exactly what they sound like: squares of fabric that are folded and tucked into the breast pocket of a tuxedo or suit jacket. There are a wide variety of pocket square folds.

The pocket square is another good opportunity to work the wedding colors into the attire. It should match or complement the tie or vest being worn, and again, the groom(s) should be different from the wedding party.

Shoes

Lastly, you need to think about shoes. Tuxedos require the fanciest of shoes: shiny black tuxedo shoes. If you don't already own a tux and are renting, you can rent shoes at the same time.

With suits, the color of the suit guides the color of the shoes. Black or charcoal suits call for black shoes. With a navy suit, you can wear either black shoes or cordovan, which is a very rich brown/burgundy color. A grey suit looks best with either black or light brown shoes. And if you choose a lighter blue (i.e., not navy) suit, light brown shoes will also look best.

Rent vs. Buy

If you think you'll have any future opportunity to wear a tuxedo, buying one for your wedding can be a smart play. Otherwise, they are easy to rent, and you don't have to worry about styles changing.

Everyone should own at least one good suit, so if your groomsmen don't already own suits, this can be a good opportunity for them to invest in something they will need for everything from job interviews to other weddings. But suits can just as easily be rented.

A few of my favorite places to send clients are Generation Tux, Men's Wearhouse, The Black Tux, and J. Hilburn. The online companies (Generation Tux and The Black Tux) will have you submit your measurements, or possibly just your height and weight to make the best attempt at sizing. (They claim to have algorithms to help with sizing, because everything is done by algorithm these days.) They will ship the suit or tuxedo far enough in advance that you have time to send it back and get another one if the sizing isn't quite right the first time.

If you are looking to have a suit made for you, most reasonably large cities have tailors and custom suiting shops designed for this purpose. Some offer fully bespoke tailoring, which means that the suit is entirely customized for you. You will undergo multiple fittings, and every detail will be chosen by you and your tailor. This is the most expensive option.

Made-to-measure is an alternative to fully bespoke. With made-to-measure, you choose from an array of pre-determined styles and fabrics, and the tailor takes initial measurements before placing the order. Once your suit arrives, it can be altered for a better fit, but the process doesn't involve the sort of minute custom fittings and measurements that bespoke does. Made-to-measure is quite a bit less expensive than bespoke.

As with wedding gowns, suits can also be purchased "off the rack." You walk into a store, try on a suit, and purchase that exact suit. It may still need alterations in order for it to fit you perfectly, but it's a less expensive option than made-to-measure.

Your Homework Assignment

Browse the internet for suit and tuxedo styles and start thinking about what you want to wear. Your venue and the time of year will help guide you. You don't want to wear a tuxedo for a beach wedding because it's too formal, and if you're getting married outside in the summer, you might want a linen suit or a light-colored suit. Decide if you want to rent or buy and make the relevant appointments. After purchasing or renting a suit or tuxedo, decide which accessories you need.

Wedding Party Attire

Back in the day, there weren't many options when it came to wedding party attire: all the ladies were going to wear the same (hideous) dress and all the guys were going to wear matching tuxedos. But we have so many more options now, and not just for the attire. Brides may have male attendants. Grooms may have some women in their wedding party. Let's cover all the options.

Attire Options for the Ladies

Dressing all the women in your wedding party has so much more flexibility than it used to, and bridesmaid dresses have come a long way since the frou-frou ruffled pastel abominations of the 1980s. Here are four routes you can take when it comes to bridesmaid attire:

1. All ladies dress in the same color but choose their own style based on their body type and what flatters them. This approach is easier if you choose a specific dress designer and a specific color from that designer and ask everyone to just pick their favorite dress in that color from that designer. This is the only way to ensure that everyone really is wearing the same shade because one designer's "claret" is another's "ruby."

2. Choose an overarching color, say, blue, and ask your attendants to dress in their preferred shade of blue. Some might be in navy, some in royal blue, and some in sky blue.

3. If you want slightly more control over the final look, you can arrange an ombré color scheme. Each person would choose their ideal shade, and then you coordinate to make sure you have the right number of people in each color/shade. For example, your maid of honor could wear burgundy, the next bridesmaid could wear deep red, then one would wear a mid-range red, and the final bridesmaid would wear pink. Option #3 is a bit more work than #2.

4. You can also ask your bridesmaids to all wear the same color but choose a different, complementary color for your maid of honor. This concept can also be achieved by giving your maid of honor a different bouquet from the other attendants.

When it comes to shoes, neutral is best. Think metallics, beige or "nude for you," or even black, depending on the color of your dresses. It's not 1987 — we're not wearing dyeable shoes in the exact shade of our dresses anymore. (Yes, that's a thing we did in the '80s.)

All your attendants should wear the same color shoe, especially if they're not wearing full-length gowns. Their shoes will be in a lot of photos, and you want them to complement each other. They don't have to wear the same style of shoe, but the same color is helpful.

And remember, ladies aren't just limited to dresses anymore. There are a lot of cute dressy jumper/romper/pantsuits out there.

Attire Options for the Guys

Guys also have many options when it comes to attire, but the groomsmen should be dressed in the same style as the groom. If the groom is wearing a suit, you don't want the groomsmen in tuxes.

1. Tuxedos. The classic. Usually black, but can also be navy, grey, burgundy, or even white. Generally, all the men wear the same color and style of tuxedo. Then the groom's tie and potentially vest are a different color than the groomsmen's. Or the groom can wear a different color jacket than the other guys.

2. Suits. Follows the same basic idea as tuxedos. If you're not wearing three-piece suits (meaning, no vest), then the tie and pocket square are your best options for differentiating the groom from the other guys.

3. Trousers with either a shirt and vest or a shirt and suspenders. A more casual look for an outdoor ranch wedding. You can wear either a vest or suspenders, but not both. You need something to attach the boutonnières to, and they will hang awkwardly if you try to pin them to a shirt.

4. Linen pants and shirts. Perfect for a beach wedding with flip-flops.

Men's shoes are actually more complicated than women's, believe it or not. There are certain shoe/suit color combinations that you want to avoid. Here's a list of which colors work together:

1. Tuxedo: shiny black shoes. Always.
2. Black or burgundy suit: black shoes.
3. Navy suit: black, brown, or burgundy/cordovan shoes.
4. Dark grey suit: black or burgundy/cordovan shoes.
5. Light grey suit: black, brown, or burgundy/cordovan shoes.
6. Tan suit: brown shoes.

Two important notes to remember: you wear a belt OR suspenders, not both. And cummerbunds are so 1980s. If someone tries to tell you that a tuxedo with a cummerbund is a good look for your wedding, run.

How to Dress Mixed-Gender Wedding Parties

Having ladies on the groom's side and guys on the bride's side is a growing trend, kicked off by same-sex couples. If this is your situation, feel free to have all the ladies dress similarly regardless of whose "side" they're on. Or you can choose to differentiate a bridesmaid from a groomsmaid (or groomswoman, or whatever clever portmanteau you want to use).

The same goes for the guys. If all the groomsmen are wearing navy suits, then it makes sense for the bridesmen to do the same. But maybe you choose a different color of tie/pocket square for the bridesmen to set them apart from the groomsmen.

Groomswomen have quite a bit of latitude in attire. They can wear dresses that match the bridesmaids' dresses. They can wear dresses that are different but complementary to the bridesmaids' dresses and the groomsmen's ties/vests/pocket squares. They can wear rompers, which are a nice hybrid between feminine and masculine style. Or they can wear menswear-style suits to match the groomsmen.

How to Dress Wedding Attendants for a Same-Sex Wedding

Just like wedding attendants for an opposite-sex wedding! You don't have to complicate this too much. Do what feels right for you and your people. Here are a few possibilities just to get your brainstorming going:

1. Two brides, all female attendants. Maybe one bride's 'maids all wear one color and the other bride's attendants all wear a different color.

2. Two brides, mixed-gender attendants. All the guys wear the same color suit, but bride 1's guys wear deep purple ties and pocket squares and her ladies wear dresses in a shade that matches the guys' ties. Bride 2's guys wear lavender ties and pocket squares and her gals wear lavender too.

3. Two brides where one is wearing a dress and the other is wearing a suit. Maybe the bride wearing a dress has all of her attendants wear dresses as well, and the bride wearing a suit has her attendants wearing pantsuits or jumpers.

4. Two grooms, all male attendants. Use different colors of accessories to differentiate everyone. Perhaps the two grooms wear the same colors,

groom 1's guys wear a different color, and groom 2's guys wear yet a different color.

5. Two grooms, mixed-gender attendants. Do something similar to option 2 above.

6. How to differentiate two grooms from each other, if they don't want to be twinsies. Different colored accessories is the easiest way. But maybe one wears a navy suit and the other wears grey. Or one wears a full black tuxedo while the other wears black pants with a white jacket.

Style is very personal, and your wedding is also very personal. So your wedding style should be a reflection of your personalities.

Your Homework Assignment

Once you've selected your wedding party members, start thinking about how you'd like them to dress. If you have any LGBTQ+ wedding party members, be sure to ask them about their attire preferences (this also applies to cisgender people who might typically dress more in the style of the opposite gender — when in doubt, always ask).

Wedding magazines and websites have almost as many bridesmaids' dresses as bridal gowns, so you can check those out at the same time. For the gents, you'll have to decide if the groomsmen and groom will wear the same tuxedo/suit with different colored accessories, or whether you want the groom to be dressed completely differently from his groomsmen.

And if you have a mixed-gender wedding party on either side, think through the options listed above to decide which way you want to go with attire.

Also determine whether it makes sense for everyone to rent or purchase their suits/tuxedos. Once you and your wedding party have decided what everyone will wear, send them the appropriate links to purchase or rent what they need.

Wedding Skincare

There's more to wedding beauty than just having your hair and makeup done. When it comes to wedding skincare, the work begins months before your wedding.

Start New Skincare Regimens Early

Do not start any new skincare treatments or products within a few weeks of your wedding. You want to do anything new at least one month before your wedding, preferably even further in advance. Your skin needs time to adjust and potentially react to any new treatments.

Facials

If you've never had a facial before and you plan to get one before your wedding, do it at least a month in advance. Even if you don't have sensitive skin, facials can cause your skin to react in an unexpected way. Some people experience breakouts, redness, or other irritation. If you have a bad reaction, you want to give your skin plenty of time to calm down before your wedding day.

If you regularly receive facials and you know how your skin reacts, judge accordingly and plan your facial for an appropriate amount of time pre-wedding. At least a week out is preferable. And don't try anything new, including aestheticians. Stick to your usual so you don't get any nasty surprises.

Makeup

If you usually don't wear a lot of makeup, you may not want to go overboard with makeup on your wedding day. A full face of makeup can feel weird if you're not used to it. If you're uncomfortable, that will show in photos. Plus, if you usually don't wear makeup but wear a lot of it on your wedding day, you may feel that your wedding photos just aren't "you."

Wedding day makeup is meant to be "more" than your everyday look, but there are ways for your makeup artist to do a natural look on you that will reflect your style while also looking good in photos.

If you do normally wear makeup, then you can feel free to amp it up a bit on your wedding day. A makeup trial is still recommended, just so you can be sure that the look you're envisioning is what you really want.

Hair

The same rules apply to hairstyles. If you wear your hair down all the time, but are thinking you want an elaborate up-do for your wedding, do a trial run to see what you think. And be sure to have someone take photos of you with your hairstyles. Some brides think they like their look, but are disappointed when they see their photos later because they don't look like themselves.

Sunscreen

Let's face it, we should all be wearing sunscreen every day. But it's especially important in the months leading up to your wedding day. This goes for your mom and your bridesmaids as well. There is nothing worse than tan lines in photos!

Tan lines can take months to fade away, so you'll need to be diligent about staying out of the sun and applying loads of sunscreen for several months. If you want to look tanned on your wedding day, a spray tan is the easy solution. They are quick, inexpensive, and easy to find. Bonus: they don't irradiate your skin.

Never get a spray tan on the day of your wedding. You will look orange. You want to do any spray tanning at least two days before your wedding. Many photos will be taken of you at your rehearsal dinner, so you need to give your tan time to settle.

And don't worry, you can shower regularly after getting a spray tan. It just needs a few hours to be set, and then a shower or two to get the initial orangeness off.

Your Homework Assignment

Consider your options when it comes to what you want to do with your hair and makeup on your wedding day. If you have any skin issues that you want to deal with, make plans for that now.

Invitations

The invitation (and save-the-date) sets the tone for your wedding. It gives your guests their first ideas of what your wedding will be like—the level of formality, the color scheme, the aesthetics.

Collecting Guest Addresses

One of the more tedious aspects of planning a wedding is collecting full names, addresses, and potentially email addresses for all your guests. As a reminder, you can use the guest list template included with this book to track all sorts of information related to your guests. You can find that template at bit.ly/ RJE-guest-list.

When using the template included with this book, you may wonder what the difference is between "Party Name," "Last Name/First Name," and "Formal Name."

The formal name is the name including the honorifics (Mr., Mrs., or Ms.). For example, Mr. & Mrs. Stephen MacDougal would be the formal name. Each person in that couple would then have their name listed in the Last Name and First Name columns. (Notice that the wife's first name doesn't appear in the formal name.)

The Party Name column is useful for guests who are coupled up but do not have the same last name. When it comes time to make your seating chart, you will want to seat couples together, but if you sort your spreadsheet by last name, people who have different last names will be separated. Sorting by party name instead will keep those couples together in the list. If a couple has different last names, choose one of the last names as the "Party Name" and assign that name to both individuals.

As I mentioned in the section about wedding websites, you may need to collect guest address information in a specific format in order to upload it to the site where you are ordering your invitations. For that reason, it can be helpful to sort out where you're ordering invitations before you dive into collecting guest information. We covered some options for where to order invitations in the previous chapter in the section about hiring a stationer or calligrapher.

When collecting guest information, you will need a first and last name for everyone on your list. Very formal invitations traditionally also included guests' middle names, but it's rare to see that in modern times. Collecting email addresses can be helpful in the event you need to communicate with everyone easily. Couples who had to postpone their weddings due to the COVID-19 pandemic found email a much easier route for communication.

We'll discuss envelope addressing in more detail after we first discuss the wording of your invitation.

Invitation Wording

Traditional invitation wording doesn't cut it for today's couple. What if there are divorced parents? Remarried parents? Two brides? No brides? Here's some advice to help you navigate your wedding invitation wording.

Back in the "old days," weddings were hosted by the bride's parents, and the invitations were issued in their names.

> Mr. & Mrs. Steven R. Smith
> Request the honour of your presence
> at the marriage of their daughter
> Suzanne Marie
> to
> Mr. Thomas L. Stevens

So what are the problems with this? Well, the groom's parents and the bride's mother aren't mentioned at all. Being "Mrs. Steven R. Smith" isn't exactly being recognized for the important role of Mother of the Bride. And what if the bride has a different last name from her parents? (It happens rather frequently.)

With the increase in the number of couples paying for all or some of their wedding themselves, not to mention marriage equality, invitation wording needs an update to modern times.

Here are a few updated options:

Both sets of parents hosting, no divorced parents:

> Steven & Marie Smith
> and
> Lawrence & Cheryl Stevens
> Request the pleasure of your company
> at the marriage of their children
> Suzanne Marie
> and
> Thomas Lawrence

Both sets of parents hosting, one set of parents divorced, not remarried:

Marie Smith and Steven Smith
with
Lawrence & Cheryl Stevens
Request the pleasure of your company
at the marriage of their children
Suzanne Marie
and
Lauren Renée

Note that the last names of the couple getting married do not appear in these versions. That's because the last names have been previously mentioned when the parents were listed.

If you have a situation where both sets of parents are divorced, or there are any remarriages, it's best to leave the parents' names off the invitation altogether. You want to keep the focus of the invitation on the couple getting married. A laundry list of parents' names will detract from that. In this version, you would use the couple's last names so all guests are aware of who, exactly, is getting married.

Example:

Together with their families
Suzanne M. Smith
and
Thomas L. Stevens
Invite you to join them
as they celebrate their marriage

Or:

Together with their parents
Suzanne Marie Smith
and
Lauren Renée Stevens
Request the pleasure of your company
at their wedding

A note on the request line: traditionally, "the honour of your presence" (British spelling) was requested for ceremonies taking place in a house of worship and "the pleasure of your company" was requested for ceremonies taking place elsewhere. "Honour of your presence" is very formal and a little stilted, so it has fallen by the wayside to some extent.

For couples whose parents are not involved in their lives or their weddings, you can dispense with the first line altogether and go directly to the couple's names:

Lawrence Thomas Stevens

and

Paul Philip McCarthy

Invite you to a celebration of their marriage

The default invitation templates on most websites still hew toward the traditional, so feel free to change them as necessary to fit your unique situation.

Envelope Addressing

Traditional wedding invitations came with two envelopes — an outer envelope where the formal titles and address were printed, and an inner envelope where just the informal names were printed. Today, it's much more common to find invitations with only the outer envelope. If this is the case, it's imperative that you find out the names of your guests' partners, because "& Guest" should never appear on an outer envelope.

Here are a few examples of how a properly addressed wedding invitation should look if there are both outer and inner envelopes. If you only have one envelope, follow the template for the outer envelope.

Example:
Outer envelope (married couple):
Mr. & Mrs. Stephen MacDougal
5436 Old Pine Lake Road
Wooster, Ohio 44278

Inner envelope:
Mr. & Mrs. MacDougal (or Stephen & Patricia to be even less formal)

Outer envelope (engaged or cohabitating couple, or a married couple with different last names):
Mr. Stephen MacDougal and Ms. Patricia Regan

5436 Old Pine Lake Road
Wooster, Ohio 44278

Inner envelope:
Mr. MacDougal & Ms. Regan (or Stephen & Patricia)

Outer envelope (long-term relationship but not living at the same address):
Mr. Stephen MacDougal
5436 Old Pine Lake Road
Wooster, Ohio 44278

Inner envelope:
Stephen & Patricia

Outer envelope (single guest who may bring a date whose name you don't know):
Mr. Stephen MacDougal
5436 Old Pine Lake Road
Wooster, Ohio 44278

Inner envelope:
Stephen & Guest

If you would prefer to be less formal in addressing your wedding invitations, leave off the honorifics (the Mr., Mrs., or Ms.) and just proper names only. For example:

Stephen & Patricia MacDougal
Stephen MacDougal & Patricia Regan (if they are married)
Stephen MacDougal
& Patricia Regan (if they are not married)
Patricia & Stephen MacDougal (if you are friends with Patricia, rather than Stephen)
Patricia Regan & Stephen MacDougal

If you only have one envelope and you don't know the name of the potential date of the person you're inviting, place a note inside letting your friend know that they're welcome to bring a guest and ask them to kindly include their guest's full name on the response card. You'll need that name for the seating chart later, and potentially to keep track of their dinner order if you're serving a pre-plated meal.

When to mail save-the-dates and wedding invitations

When it comes time to begin letting guests know about your wedding, you might be wondering when the best time is to mail your save-the-dates and your wedding invitations. For save-the-dates, there's no one-size-fits-all answer, so I'll start there.

When to send save-the-dates

Sending save-the-date cards is a relatively new wedding tradition. Until a decade or so ago, this was not a thing. People just received a wedding invitation and then decided whether or not to attend. Simple!

But weddings are getting more elaborate, and friends and family are becoming more far-flung, requiring more people to travel to attend any given wedding. With that in mind, an informal notification to guests that a wedding will be held months in the future gives people extra time to arrange their schedules and travel accommodations.

How far in advance to send a save-the-date depends on your wedding location and guest list.

- For an international destination wedding, send save-the-dates at least one year in advance. International travel is difficult and expensive, so your guests will need plenty of time to plan.

- For a domestic destination wedding (Hawaii, a ranch in Montana, a ski resort in Vermont), 10-12 months before the wedding would be a good time to send save-the-dates.

- If many of your guests will have to travel to your wedding, regardless of where it's being held, 6-8 months' notice will be appreciated. That gives people enough advance notice to block off time on their calendars (especially for a summer wedding when family vacations may conflict).

- If you are getting married in your hometown, where you still live, and where most of your friends and family also live, you can get away without save-the-dates at all. But if you still want to send them, 6 months out from the wedding is standard.

If you are planning your wedding in a short time-frame (six month or less) send save-the-dates as soon as humanly possible. Don't wait until you book a photographer, have an engagement photo session, get the photos back from the photographer, order printed save-the-date cards, receive them, and then mail them. You don't have that kind of time!

Electronic save-the-dates are also perfectly acceptable, regardless of whether you're in a time crunch. Paperless Post has some really cute options. You'll just need to gather email addresses for everyone on your guest list.

One important piece of information to include on your save-the-dates is the URL for your wedding website. Even if there's no information on the website yet, you should still include the URL. That way guests can check back and get the information they need for travel, sending a gift, and attending the wedding.

When to send the wedding invitation

To figure out when to mail your wedding invitations, you need to work backwards from your wedding date. Your caterer and venue will want your final head count anywhere from 10 to 21 days before your wedding. Some people will forget to respond to your invitation, so you need to allow yourself time to track down RSVP stragglers.

Setting an RSVP deadline of 2 weeks before your final headcount is due will give you time to follow up with anyone who didn't respond to the invitation. But you also need to give people a little bit of time between when they receive the invitation and when they respond.

It's best not to give people too much time to let an invitation sit around, so you want them to have the invitation about a month before they have to reply. This means you should mail invitations about 8-10 weeks before your wedding date.

- Example wedding date: October 10
- Final head count due: September 26
- RSVP deadline: September 12
- Mail invitations: between August 1 and 15

Change-the-date cards

If you find yourself needing to reschedule your wedding, change-the-date cards are now everywhere, thanks to the COVID-19 pandemic. You can order printed cards to match your original invitation suite, send electronic notices, or even just send an email. You should send out your change-the-date notice as soon as you know what your new date is. If you need to move your wedding to an undetermined future date, you can send cards to let guests know the wedding has been postponed and that the new date will be announced as soon as you have one.

Your Homework Assignment

First, figure out whether you want to include parents' names on the invitation or not. If your parents are hosting or contributing a large amount of money, you should check with them. They may expect to be listed.

Next, decide on the level of formality of your invitation wording. Will you be requesting the honour of their presence, or the pleasure of their company?

Next, begin browsing online invitation sites or schedule a meeting with your stationer if you're going the custom route. Be sure to create an account and log into it before you start browsing so you can easily save favorites to come back to later. Remember your overall design aesthetic and color scheme as you are browsing. Anything that doesn't fit shouldn't be favorited.

Finalize your invitation choice and decide which additional pieces you will need, such as response cards, direction cards, reception cards, brunch invitations, or map cards. Most invitation suites come with matching thank you notes, return address labels, save-the-dates, and a variety of other items.

Guest Book

A wedding guest book is exactly what it sounds like: a book where all your wedding guests can sign their names and write you a little note of well-wishes. But it doesn't have to be an actual book! These days there are so many interesting wedding guest book options.

An Actual Book

If you do still want to use an actual book as your wedding guest book, Etsy has approximately 1 million possibilities. You can find books that have wood covers, books with acrylic covers, books with traditional covers. The cover can be carved, engraved, or embossed with your names, your initials, your wedding date—pretty much anything you want.

Your Engagement Photos

One of the reasons I recommend having engagement photos taken is that you can make use of them at your wedding, especially as a guest book. Here are four ideas for how to use your engagement photos as a guest book:

1. Choose a few of your favorites, take them to your local frame shop and have them custom matted. Guests sign the mat around the photos, and then you take it back to the shop to have it framed under glass.

2. Choose your favorite photo and have it enlarged to poster size (18x24 or 24x36). Your guests will sign on the photo itself, and then you can hang it as-is or have it framed under glass for display.

3. Choose your favorite photo and have it enlarged to poster size, then framed under glass. Your guests will sign ON the glass using special markers.

4. Create a photo book using Shutterfly or another online photo book printing service. Leave plenty of white space on the pages so your guests can sign.

Other Creative Options

I've seen every single one of these ideas in action, either at clients' weddings or at friends' weddings.

- Small wooden hearts that guests sign and then drop into a glass-front box through a slit in the top.
- Wooden puzzle pieces that fit together to form a heart.

- An Up-themed poster with the house and a bunch of balloon strings pre-printed. Guests use ink pads to leave their thumbprint at the end of balloon strings, so their thumbprint becomes the balloon. Super cute! (But use caution—stray ink marks can be a problem.)
- Jenga pieces.
- An atlas or world map, and guests sign in places where they recommend you travel and visit.
- Paper butterflies that are then glued onto a board and framed, creating 3D wall art.
- Typewritten notes made on a vintage typewriter.
- Instax instant cameras are super popular right now, but they need a lot of instruction for guests to know what to do. Some couples want guests to take their selfie, write a note on the front, and then tape the photos into a book. Some couples want guests to take a selfie, write a note on either the front or back, and then clip them to a wire-strung frame. And some couples want guests to take two selfies: one to keep, and one to leave behind in the guest book. Be sure to make whatever signage you need to instruct your guests.
- The end of a barrel (wine, bourbon, or other).
- A large wooden sign with the couple's names and wedding date, or new last name.
- A large wooden letter (whatever the first letter of the couple's last name is).
- An illustration with lots of white space for guests to sign. The illustration can be of the couple, or their venue, or their home state, or both of their home states if they're from different states.

Important Tips

Be sure to buy pens that are labeled either "archival" or "acid-free" so that the ink won't degrade over time. Have a little pen jar or caddy next to the guest book to help corral pens. They often roll off the table if left scattered. Purchase at least four pens and as many as a full dozen, depending on how many people you expect at your wedding. Sometimes guests accidentally walk off with the pens.

Place your guest book on a table near the entrance of your venue so that guests can sign as they arrive before the ceremony. Then have your wedding coordinator move the guest book during the ceremony so that it's near the cocktail hour area. That way guests who arrived late or forgot to sign earlier can sign during cocktail hour.

If your wedding is being held outdoors, ask your coordinator to remove the guest book after dusk so that the change in temperature or humidity doesn't do any damage. Bring your guest book in its original box so it can be packed in the same box at the end of the wedding. Keep any protective packing material intact.

If you are framing something under glass, ask for UV-filtering glass to prevent sun damage. Never hang or display your guest book at home anywhere that the sun will shine on it regularly.

Your Homework Assignment

Decide what you want to do for a guest book. Start browsing online or thinking about making one yourself. Order your guest book at least two months before your wedding so you don't have to worry about shipping delays.

Signage

When it comes to your wedding, you want to have as much signage as necessary to make things easier for your guests. If there's any information you want them to have, wedding signage is the way to communicate it. Here's a complete list of all the signage you might want to incorporate.

The Wedding Signage You Might Want

1. **Directional and way-finding.** Are the restrooms difficult to find? Put up a sign. Are the ceremony and reception in opposite directions when people first enter the property? Signage can help!

2. **Welcome.** A large sign on an easel is a popular way to welcome guests to your wedding. It can be as straightforward as "Welcome to Our Wedding," or "Welcome to Our Forever." Often the couple's names and the wedding date are listed as well. Some couples opt for wording that will allow them to hang the piece in their new home. For example, "The Watsons | October 19, 2019" or something similar.

3. **Unplugged ceremony.** As cell phones become more ubiquitous, it's becoming more common for couples to ask their guests to put away their phones during the ceremony—not just to silence them, but to avoid using them to take photos or videos. You hired professionals to handle the photography; you don't need a bunch of photos of your guests taking photos with their phones. Pinterest and Etsy are full of examples of signage wording that you can use to request an unplugged ceremony.

4. **Open ceremony seating.** Traditionally, the bride's friends and family sat on the left side of the church (or aisle) and the groom's friends and family sat on the right. This has mostly gone by the wayside, and most couples opt for open seating. But many guests will still ask which side they should sit on. You can avoid this with signage indicating that seating is open. Two clever, rhyming approaches are "Choose a seat, not a side, we're all family once the knot is tied" and "Pick a seat, not a side, you're loved by both the groom and bride."

5. **Reserved ceremony seating.** If there are particular seats you'd like to assign at the ceremony (such as the parents of the couple), you can create individual cards to hang on those chairs. At the very least, I recommend having 2–4 "Reserved" signs to hang on the chairs in the

first row (or first two rows) on each side, depending on how many immediate family members you'd like to have priority seating.

6. **Cards and gifts.** Not many people bring gifts to weddings these days because online registries make it easier to have the gift mailed directly to the couple. But it's still helpful to have some space for gifts. And most guests still bring cards, so having a card box or basket is essential. A simple sign that says "Cards" will tell your guests where to put their card.

7. **Guest book.** If your guest book is an actual book for guests to sign, you can probably get away without any signage. Most people are going to be able to figure that out. But if it's anything else, signage and instructions are helpful. Maybe it's a map or atlas and you want guests to sign in their favorite vacation destination. Maybe it's a photo book of engagement photos and you want them to sign the pages. Maybe it's a set of blank puzzle pieces. Maybe you're using the popular Instax instant cameras and you want guests to paste their photos into a book. Whatever it is, provide some guidance so they know what they're doing.

8. **Table and seat assignments.** If you have totally open seating at your reception (not recommended), then you don't need any seating signage. The most common option is to assign guests to specific tables. You can do a large seating chart, either printed on foam board or hand-lettered on a mirror. You can do individual "escort cards" that are displayed on a table. Or you can combine the escort card with a take-home favor, such as a small plant, a jar of honey, or a caramel apple. The tag on the favor would have guests' names and tables numbers on it. If you've assigned seats at the tables, then you will also need cards at each seat with the guests' names on them, called place cards. It's very common at weddings these days to only use escort cards and allow the guests to arrange themselves at the table. Very formal events continue to use both escort and place cards, and some caterers require them for pre-plated meals. But if you want to save yourself a little time and trouble (and money on stationery and calligraphy), just use escort cards or a seating chart and skip the place cards.

9. **Table numbers or names.** This one is self-explanatory. The guests need to know which tables are which.

10. **Bar menu.** List out your signature cocktails if you have them, or the types of liquor available if it's a full bar. List the types of wine and beer

on offer. You might also consider listing the non-alcoholic beverages available.

11. **Dessert table.** If your caterer is putting together a dessert buffet, they will probably have signage to indicate what's what. But if you've ordered multiple desserts from a bakery, or multiple flavors of cupcakes, you'll want to order signage to display. You may also consider a sign that says something like, "Please wait until after dinner to taste," to avoid people raiding the dessert buffet before the proper time.

12. **Wedding favors.** If you're giving guests a take-home favor, you might consider signage. If the favors were the escort cards or are placed at individual guest seats, then signage isn't necessary. But if the favors are all staged together in a central location, something to indicate that guests should take one is advised.

Where to Get Wedding Signage

Etsy is full of templates for DIY signs. In some cases, you'll be able to print the signs yourself—think bar menus, favor signs, table numbers, cards/gifts, and favor signage. But for the larger signs like the welcome, unplugged, and directional signage, you'll probably need to send it out. Specialty printers are ideal for this type of work, but your local FedEx or UPS Store should also be able to help you.

For smaller signs, you'll want to frame them in something that can stand up by itself. Don't use flimsy paper, or even cardstock, unless you plan to put it inside a frame. For your larger signs, cardstock is not sufficiently sturdy to stand up against any potential wind. You'll want "foam core" board (or the even sturdier "gator board") or wood for your large signs.

Browse through Pinterest to get some ideas on wording. I recommend creating a section on your wedding Pinterest board just for signage so you can easily keep track of them.

Many rental companies also can provide signage for the non-personalized items, such as unplugged ceremony, open ceremony seating, cards/gifts, favors, and directional signage.

You can also have signage custom-made by a calligrapher or hand-letterer for the most personalized, elegant look. Many calligraphers have rental items such as mirrors that they can write on for your wedding, then remove the writing and use them again for future weddings. If your calligraphy uses acrylic signage, be sure they're using sturdy acrylic. If it bends easily, it's not sturdy enough. I don't recommend signs on glass because it's too fragile.

How to Display Your Wedding Signage

Large signs are best displayed on easels. Check with your venue to see if they have easels available. Your calligrapher may also have them to rent, or your event rental company.

Smaller signage can be displayed either on a tabletop easel, or in a picture frame with a stand, or just propped up against something. When you think through which signage you want, also consider how you will display it.

Keep in mind the usual weather patterns for your geographic location. If your wedding is being held outside, and afternoon winds usually pick up right around the time of your wedding, your signage will need to be sturdy so it doesn't blow away.

Your Homework Assignment

Using the list above, decide which signage you want or need for your wedding. Make a list. Start browsing Etsy for ideas and save your favorites. Consider which items need to be custom-made (like a welcome sign with your names) and which ones can be more generic (like table numbers). Local calligraphers usually also do signage. You'll save on shipping if you order your signs locally.

Order everything but your escort cards, place cards, and table numbers as you decide what you want. You won't know how many tables you have, who is coming, or where they are sitting until much closer to the wedding. But don't save everything for the last minute.

Seating Assignments

When people attend a wedding, they generally expect to be told where to sit — a table assignment at least, if not a seat assignment. Who tells them where to sit? You do.

There are basically four steps to making your seating assignments.

1. Finalize Your Attendee List

You can't make a seating chart until you know who's coming to your wedding. And making a seating chart is time-consuming and kind of a pain. So make sure your RSVP deadline on your wedding invitations is well in advance of your wedding date. I recommend making the deadline a full month before the wedding date to give you time to track down stragglers who don't RSVP at all. (Also because your caterer will want your final count about two weeks before your wedding.)

The day after your RSVP deadline, begin contacting anyone who didn't reply. Maybe they didn't receive the invitation. Maybe you didn't receive their reply. Maybe they haven't figured out yet whether they can make it. You will need a final answer from everyone no more than one week after your RSVP deadline.

2. Make Your Floor Plan

Proximity to the couple getting married is a sign of status when it comes to wedding seating. You can't figure out which tables are going to be closest to you until you have a floor plan. Some venues will provide the floor plan and lay out the tables for you. In some cases, you may have to rely on your wedding planner to help you.

If you don't have a wedding planner, you're on your own here. If your venue doesn't make the layout for you, they might at least have a blank template of their space that you can draw tables on to get some idea of where they will go. "Close enough" counts here. Don't stress too much about getting the placement exact.

3. Number the Tables

It's very important that you do this step BEFORE you begin assigning guests to tables. Imagine that you're walking into a room full of tables, and you know you're at table 12, but you don't know where table 12 is. It will be much easier for you to find it if the tables are positioned in numerical order. If you see table 9 and then 10, you'll know you're on the right track.

But imagine walking into a room where table 10 is next to table 3, and table 11 is next to table 5. It makes no sense! Don't do that to your guests.

If half your tables are on one side and half on the other side with the dance floor in the middle, number all the tables on one side in order, then start where you left off and number the tables on the other side in order. So, for example, tables 1-4 would be on the left, and tables 5-8 would be on the right. Here's what it looks like:

Table 1		Table 5
Table 2	Dance	Table 6
Table 3	Floor	Table 7
Table 4		Table 8

4. Assign Guests to Tables

Now that you know who is coming, where the tables are located, and which tables are which, you're finally ready to assign people to tables. Begin with the easy guests: your parents and immediate family members. Generally, each set of parents will have their table near the couple's table, regardless of whether the couple is doing a sweetheart table (just the two of them) or a head table (the couple plus their wedding party members). If you're dealing with divorced parents, then each parent should have their own table. Your parents may have ideas about who they want to sit with. Maybe it's their siblings, maybe it's their other children, maybe it's close friends. Ask them what they want in order to make things easier on yourself.

Some rules to consider when assigning tables:

- always seat people with their spouse or date for the evening; never split up couples;

- think about people who have things in common, will get along, and will have interesting conversations — seat those people at the same table, even if they don't already know each other;

- 60" round tables comfortably seat 8 people, but you can squeeze in 10 if necessary;

- 72" round tables comfortably seat 10 people, 12 if you squeeze;

- 6' banquet or farm tables comfortably seat six people (three on each long side); most rental companies will tell you they seat 8, but it's tight because of the way the legs work;

- try not to have fewer than 6 people at a table or it will feel sparse;

- consider a kids' table if you have a lot of kids aged 5-10; provide activity books to keep them occupied;
- if you're assigning seats in addition to tables, try to alternate men with women.

Give yourself at least two weeks to complete the seating assignments. If you're having individual escort cards printed or hand-calligraphed, you might need even more time. Check with your calligrapher to find out what their turn-around time is.

If you're printing a large seating chart, remember that you need time to input all the data into the template and then get the file to a printer to be printed on large-format foam board. DO NOT wait until the last minute to work on your seating assignments.

Your Homework Assignment

Follow the steps above. Give yourself plenty of time for printing or calligraphy of final seating assignments.

Gifts, Favors, and Welcome Bags

As a couple getting married, you will invariably receive gifts from your friends and family. But there are a few people to whom you should be giving gifts: each other, your parents, and your wedding party attendants.

Gifts to Each Other

It's traditional for a couple getting married to give each other something special and meaningful as a wedding gift. It should be personal and should remind your spouse of the love you share and this very special experience of your wedding day.

Often, jewelry, watches, and cuff links are lovely choices, if those are appropriate for your new spouse. If your fiancé(e) doesn't wear French cuff shirts, then cuff links are probably not a great choice. I recommend avoiding consumable items, such as perfume and cologne, because you want something that they can cherish forever.

You should hopefully know each other better than anyone, so only you can choose the perfect gift for your new spouse. Put your heart into it, and you will come up with something perfect.

Gifts for Your Parents

Typically, the wedding couple gives gifts to their parents to thank them for their years of love and support—and possibly for financial support with the wedding. A classic parent gift is a very nice photo frame, silver or something similarly elegant. Later, when the wedding photos come back, your parents can choose their favorite and you can buy them a print to put in the frame.

The parent gifts are usually a joint gift: from both of you to both of your parents, and from both of you to both of your spouse's parents. If any of the parents are divorced, then you'll obviously need separate gifts.

As with the gifts you give each other, think about what would be special and meaningful to your parents. It's easier if you give each set of parents the same or a similar gift, but if not, they should be gifts of a similar price.

Gifts for Your Wedding Party

If you have a large wedding party, this category can add up fast. You'll want gifts for your maid of honor/best man, bridesmaids, groomsmen, flower girls, and ring bearers. Plus your officiant, if it's a friend or family member performing your ceremony.

Classic gifts for ladies include pashminas, silk robes, a piece of inexpensive jewelry, a monogrammed tote bag, or monogrammed stemless wine glasses.

For the guys, monogrammed catch-all trays, utility knives, whiskey tasting glasses, or ties and pocket squares are popular choices.

Those are all clearly very gender-normative. Again, think about your attendants and what makes sense for them. If you and your best girlfriends are all whiskey drinkers, then maybe get them some engraved whiskey glasses.

When to Deliver the Gifts

The best time to exchange gifts with your spouse-to-be is the night before your wedding. On your wedding day, you will be busy and at the end of the day, you will be tired. Treat wedding eve like Christmas Eve and exchange gifts in a quiet moment together.

When it comes to both the gifts for your parents and the gifts for your attendants, the best time to give them is at the rehearsal dinner. Everyone is gathered in one place, and you can make a little thank you speech to go along with presenting the gifts.

However, if your rehearsal dinner is very large and includes all of the out-of-town guests attending your wedding, you may not want to give these gifts there. In that case, I recommend giving your attendants their gifts on the wedding day when you are all getting ready together. And your parents' gifts should be given at a quiet moment the night before your wedding. You and your partner should give the parent gifts together, because they are from both of you.

Favors

Take-home favors for guests are more common in some areas of the country than in others. There are a few different ways to handle favors, if you decide to do them.

Typically, favors are placed at a central location with a sign noting that guests should "please take one" on their way out. If you want to be certain each guest knows about the favors, you might consider placing a favor at each place setting. You'll need either your caterer or your coordinator to do this for you.

Common favor items include olive oil, honey, sea salt, cookies, chocolates, Jordan almonds, coffee, coasters, bottle openers, small plants, custom-designed place cards, playing cards—the list goes on. They are generally small and not crazy expensive.

Within the past several years, a charitable donation in lieu of favors has become common. You may choose to print individual cards to place at each place setting, or (to save paper) you might wish to have a sign placed somewhere in the reception, or even one sign per table.

Some couples opt to do both take-home favors and a charitable donation. And some couples do neither. It's a matter of personal choice (and budget).

Wedding Welcome Bags

If you've ever traveled for a wedding, chances are good that when you arrived at your hotel, you were handed a wedding welcome bag put together for you by the couple. But if you've never experienced this, you might be wondering what a welcome bag is and what should go in it.

The wedding welcome bag is exactly what it sounds like—a little bag of goodies to welcome your guests to your wedding weekend. It's a little way of saying, "Hi, we're glad you're here. Here are a few things to make your stay more enjoyable!"

What to include in the wedding welcome bag

- Bottled water (one bottle per person); you can have custom labels made, but it's perfectly fine not to.
- "Hangover remedy" kit, including ibuprofen, antacids, maybe Gatorade. You can buy these kits pre-made.
- Snacks—chips, granola bars, chocolate bars. If the city where you're getting married is known or famous for a particular food item, it's a nice touch to include that.
- List of things to do in the area. This doesn't have to be elaborate. Items to include: favorite restaurants and bars, museums, the zoo, wine-tasting, other popular activities.
- Schedule of events for the weekend, if there's more happening than just the wedding ceremony and reception. If you've arranged any group outings or tours, include them here.
- A hand-drawn map of the property and the various locations of events taking place, if this applies to your wedding. You can have an artist draw the map and then reproduce it in bulk.
- Sunscreen, lip balm, inexpensive sunglasses, or flip-flops for weddings taking place during summer or near the beach.
- A bottle of wine.
- Tea sachets or fancy coffee.

What to put it all in

You can get as elaborate as you want to with this. Typically, you would just use a small paper shopping bag with handles. You can buy them in a color to complement your wedding, or just go with white. You can have a custom stamp made (your initials, your wedding date, your wedding hashtag) and stamp each bag for a personalized touch. Put a bit of tissue paper in the top to jazz it up a bit.

You can also buy canvas tote bags if you have a larger amount of items that you want to include. The advantage of canvas tote bags is that they're re-useable. But your guests may not want to re-use them if they have your names on them, so limit your personalization if you go this route.

If you want to take your welcome to the next level, you can prepare a basket or box for your guests. But this will start to get expensive fast, so you may only want to go this route if you have a very small guest list or have an unlimited budget.

How to distribute the welcome bags

If all of your out-of-town guests are staying in the same one or two hotels, you can ask the hotel to distribute the bags. Most of them will do this for a fee of several dollars per bag. They usually keep all the bags at the front desk and pass them out as guests check in. (Why they think this is worth charging several dollars per bag is beyond me.)

If you don't want to pay the hotel to do this, you can pass out the bags at a welcome party or the rehearsal dinner, but that's awkward if not everyone is getting a welcome bag. You could also ask a friend to individually take them to people's hotel rooms, but then they would have to know which room everyone is staying in, and there's a chance the guests would not be in the room to accept delivery.

If many of your guests are making their own arrangements and staying in Airbnbs, you may wish to forego the welcome bag because distribution would be very challenging in that case.

Remember this key rule of wedding planning: don't take anything on if it's just going to cause you more stress than it's worth. Wedding welcome bags are a nice touch and will be appreciated by your guests. But if you can't make the logistics work, then skip it.

Your Homework Assignment

Make a list of everyone you want to give a gift to. Set a budget for each category (you may spend more on your parents than on your wedding party). Brainstorm ideas and write them down. Order gifts with enough lead time to wrap them before the rehearsal dinner.

Decide whether you will provide welcome bags for out-of-town guests. If so, brainstorm ideas for what to include and purchase those items, along with bags and tissue paper. Assemble these as soon as your final guest count is known and you know how many out-of-town guests you'll have.

Registries

One of the most fun wedding planning tasks is putting together your wedding registry. It's basically a shopping spree without spending any money! But there are some helpful tips you should know before you head to the store to pick up that bar-code gun.

Registering does not need to be done right away

When you first get engaged, there's a flurry of activity as you try to choose a date, find a venue, and book all your important service providers (planner, caterer, photographer, DJ, florist). Don't add registering to that list. Wait until things calm down a bit.

One benchmark to follow is to have at least one wedding registry completed before you send out your save-the-dates (if you're sending save-the-dates). You will put your wedding website on the save-the-date, and people are likely to check out your website soon after receiving notification of your wedding. If you have at least some registry information on there, it's helpful to your guests.

But it's certainly acceptable to send your save-the-dates before your wedding registries are complete. That page of your website can be "under construction" and people will check back later.

A note about registry etiquette

Although it's fine to put your wedding website on your save-the-date (in fact, it's expected), you should not put registry information directly on the save-the-date. Nor should it ever appear on a wedding invitation. The only place where registry information is proper and expected is on a shower invitation.

This is because gifts are generally expected as part of a bridal shower. Although it's typical for wedding guests to send a gift to the couple, it's considered unseemly to *ask* for gifts, which is what's implied by putting registry information on the invitation.

Think about what you need

Traditionally, couples getting married would be starting a household together for the first time and would have been living with their parents before marriage. So they needed all the household essentials: towels, sheets, china, silverware, glasses, cooking utensils, and appliances. This is not necessarily true today when couples get married at a later age, often live on their own before marriage, and often cohabitate with their significant other before marriage.

So you and your spouse-to-be should sit down and think about what you actually need. Maybe you have all the basics covered but they're kind of a mishmash of stuff that's been accumulated separately and together over the years. In that case, you might want to start fresh with all new everything.

Many couple these days do not register for fine china, knowing that they'll never use it. Similarly, if you don't expect to be throwing dinner parties for 10–12 people, you probably don't need 10–12 of everything. Think about what fits your life and your living space. A couple living in a house in the suburbs of Wisconsin can fit a lot more stuff than a couple living in a loft apartment in San Francisco.

If you don't want or need housewares, you can register for something more out-of-the-ordinary. Home décor, for example, or camping/outdoor equipment, or even booze!

And if you really don't want any stuff, then you can start a honeymoon registry. You'll allocate specific amounts to certain items. Say, $50 for a dinner out. Or $100 toward hotel nights and $25 for transportation needs. Then guests can contribute whatever they'd like and you can have a lovely honeymoon without adding to the budget burden of your wedding. Zola, Traveler's Joy, and Honeyfund are some examples of honeymoon registry sites. Be sure to compare fees among the sites before choosing one.

Where to register

You'll want to create multiple registries at a mix of stores that have different price points. Two to three registries should be sufficient, but more than four would be unwieldy. The more guests you're inviting, the more items you'll need on your registries.

Keep in mind that people will be giving you gifts both for the wedding and at your shower, so choose items at a mix of price points. Go ahead and put the $350 KitchenAid stand mixer on there, but make sure you have some $10 kitchen utensils as well.

You'll want to keep tabs on the registries as you go, to be sure you have enough items remaining for people to buy. You can always add items if things are looking sparse. Remember that some people will send gifts prior to the wedding, while others will wait until afterwards. Guests have a year after the wedding to send a gift. (You, however, do NOT have a year to write thank you notes. Those should be written and sent immediately after receiving the gift, but no later than three months after receiving the gift.)

Some popular choices for wedding registries are Crate & Barrel, Sur la Table, Pottery Barn, Williams-Sonoma, Macy's, Bed Bath & Beyond, Target, Amazon, West Elm, Anthropologie, and REI.

Some registry item ideas

Here are some registry suggestions to get you started.

A Versatile Stand Mixer

This might seem a bit old fashioned, but the stand mixer continues to be a staple in the kitchen. You can use it for a variety of cooking and baking tasks, and if you plan to host parties or holiday dinners, it's practically a must-have. Unlike a hand-held mixer, you can leave a stand mixer running on its own while you add more ingredients, or just let it do its thing. With enough counter space in your kitchen, you can leave it out full-time so it's always easy to access when you need it.

A Quality Vacuum Cleaner

No matter what your housing situation is, you're going to need a vacuum cleaner. These tend to be pricey, so they're a great registry item for your friends to go in on together. Consider your current and future needs. If you live in a house with stairs, something that's lightweight enough to carry up and down those stairs is clutch. If you have a mix of carpeting and hard flooring, be sure to look for a model that can handle both. You might even want to consider a combination wet-dry vacuum. And if you have pets, be sure to choose a model that can handle pet hair.

Well-Made Bedding

Quality sheets, blankets, duvets, and pillows can be expensive, so your wedding registry is a great opportunity to spruce up your bedroom. You'll probably want two different complete sets—one for warmer months and one for colder months. You could even consider flannel bedding if it gets really cold where you live. A complete set generally consists of a fitted sheet, a flat sheet, two pillow cases, a duvet cover, two pillow sham covers, and perhaps even a duvet (if you live in an area that calls for different warmth levels of your duvet/comforter during different times of the year).

The Right Mattress

Something else to consider including on your list is a mattress. As you begin your life with your new spouse, it's great to start off with a quality mattress that fits both of your needs. The right mattress, when paired with quality bedding, can really help elevate your quality of sleep and intimacy. Also, when is the last time you bought a new mattress? If it was more than 10 years ago, you're definitely due for a new one.

New Luggage

Your first trip together as newlyweds is likely to be your honeymoon. You'll need luggage! Even if you don't have any immediate plans to travel, quality luggage is a great registry item. Chances are that you'll eventually need to travel somewhere, and you don't want to be left scrambling for ways to transport your belongings. Splurge and request a great set of luggage that will last for many years to come. Most luggage brands these days offer far more interesting colors than black. You and your spouse can each choose your favorite color, and bonus: it will be much easier to find your bags at baggage claim.

Date Box Subscription Service

To help keep the excitement and romance alive after marriage, it will be important to make romance and dates a priority. Subscription services allow you to have custom dates-in-a-box delivered to your front door. Each month you'll get a new experience, from cooking a new meal at home, to arts and crafts, to exploring local spots. This could be a fun tradition for you and your partner, and something to look forward to each month.

Your Homework Assignment

Start a shared document where you and your fiancé(e) can both add items you think you need as you think of them. Once you have a good list going, figure out where the best stores are to get those items. (For example, if you've both listed a bunch of outdoor gear, register at REI or LL Bean, rather than Williams-Sonoma.)

Get on the email list for your chosen stores and start a registry online, even if you only put a couple things on it to start. That way they'll know to email you about any special registry events they're holding.

Complete your registry at a couple of stores and make a note of any custom URLs they provide. These will be useful for your wedding website and your shower invitations.

Track your registry from time to time to make sure there are still a variety of items on them. Add items as necessary.

Linens

Weddings require you to do a lot of things you've probably never done before, like figuring out how many tablecloths you need to order, and what size they need to be.

Almost every table at your wedding will need a tablecloth, unless you are using nice, wood farm tables, which shouldn't be covered up. In the wedding business, we refer to tablecloths and napkins as "linens," even though they are not always made of linen. The most common material is a polyester blend because it's fairly easy to clean and maintain. You can get linens in actual linen, or silk, or cotton, but they are more expensive.

Who orders the wedding linens?

In some cases, your venue or caterer may provide linens for your event. But if they do, you are likely to be limited in color choice. Often they have white and maybe one other option, like ivory or black. But if white is what you want, and they're included anyway, then go for it!

It's also possible that your caterer will manage your linen rental as part of their larger rental order of plates, flatware, glassware, etc. Most full-service catering companies will do this because they have relationships with rental companies and can get discounts not available to you as the average consumer.

Your wedding planner can also manage your rental order and potentially offer you a discounted rate. This isn't the type of service that a coordinator usually provides, but a full-service planner will.

But if you are the one who has to figure out your linen situation, you basically have two choices: rent or buy. Inexpensive tablecloths can be found on the Internet. You might be tempted to buy them thinking you will be able to resell them after the wedding. (Because let's be honest, what are you going to do with 15 120" white polyester tablecloths?)

Buying vs. Renting

I recommend NOT buying your linens for several reasons. First, you have to place your order with sufficient lead time to receive it before your wedding. Which means you need to know how many you need, which is based on how many guest tables you have, which is based on how many guests are coming. People are notoriously bad at RSVP'ing to weddings on time, so you could find yourself in need of extra linens with no time to get them. A rental company will generally let you make changes to your order up to a week before your wedding.

Another problem with buying linens is that they will be folded, wrapped in plastic, and shipped to you in a cardboard box. They will arrive heavily creased from being folded for possibly many months. If you want your linens to look good on your tables, you'll need to find the time to remove them all from the plastic bags and iron them before the wedding. (Trust me when I tell you that you are not going to have time to do this.) Rented linens will be delivered to your venue freshly laundered and pressed, on dry-cleaning hangers to prevent creases. Much better.

Then you have to worry about the end of the night. You'll have to gather up all the tablecloths, take them home, launder them, press them, package them, list them for sale, and ship them to whomever buys them (if anyone does). This is a lot of work.

Not to mention that linens take a beating at a wedding. People spill wine and drinks all over them. You'd be amazed at the amount of cake that gets ground into tablecloths. You may not be able to get some of them clean enough for resale. If you rent, you just bag up the linens at the end of the night, the rental company picks them up, launders and presses them, and gets them ready for the next client. No fuss for you!

Which tables do you need linens for?

- All guest tables
- Head table or sweetheart table
- Cocktail tables (low or hi-tops)
- Cake table
- Favor display table (not applicable if you're putting favors out at the guests' place settings)
- Escort card table (not applicable if you have a large seating chart on an easel)
- Card/gift table
- Guestbook table (might be combined with card/gift table)
- Buffet or hors d'oeuvres tables (check with your caterer)
- Bar (check with your bar manager)
- DJ (check with your DJ—some have booths as part of their set up, some use regular banquet tables)

What size tablecloths do you need?

There are a few standard table sizes: 60" round, 72" round, 6' banquet, 8' banquet, 30" round cocktail, 36" round cocktail. Here are the linen sizes for each, keeping in mind that you want the linen to go all the way down to the ground. You never want your tablecloth to be too short, exposing the table's legs.

- 60" round — 120" linen
- 72" round — 132" linen
- 36" round — 96" linen
- 36" hi-top — 132" linen (a hi-top is further from the ground, so you need a longer tablecloth)
- 6' banquet — 90" x 132"
- 8' banquet — 90" x 156" (the width of the table is the same as a 6-foot; only the length changes)

Your Homework Assignment

Keeping your color scheme in mind, start thinking about what color you might want your linens to be. You might choose one color for guest tables and a different color for accent tables (like the cake, guest book, and dessert table). Sparkly sequined tablecloths are a good choice for sweetheart and cake tables, so keep that in mind too.

Once you know how many guest dining tables you'll have, make your complete list of how many linens you need and what size.

Hotel Room Blocks

If you've ever gone to an out-of-town wedding, you may have stayed in a hotel where the couple arranged a room block for their guests. Now you're getting married, and you want to set up a hotel room block too. But how?

Setting up a hotel room block is not that difficult, but if you've never done it before, there are some tips and tricks you should know, and some terminology that will be foreign to you. If you've hired a full-service wedding planner, they'll probably handle this task for you. But if you're on your own, follow these steps.

Find one or two local hotels

You'll want to choose hotels that are reasonably close to your wedding venue. It makes transportation easier, whether you're arranging group transportation or letting guests drive themselves to and from the wedding.

If you have rewards status with a particular hotel chain, then you probably want to set up a room block there. You may get extra perks, and you might also be able to earn points.

Choose hotels that are in the proper budgetary range for your guests. Just because you usually stay in a luxury 5-star hotel when you travel doesn't mean all your guests will be able to.

Call the hotels at their local number

This is important: don't call the toll-free reservations number. You want to call the local number and speak to someone who is physically present at the property. Worldwide reservations agents can't appropriately help you with setting up a hotel room block.

Decide on a guaranteed or courtesy block

The hotel will ask if you want to set up a guaranteed or a courtesy room block. Chances are, you want a courtesy block.

With a guaranteed room block, the hotel takes your requested number of rooms out of circulation, and you guarantee that they will be booked. If you block 20 rooms, but only 15 of them are booked by your guests, you pay for the extra 5 rooms. A guaranteed room block is also sometimes called an "attrition" block.

With a courtesy room block, the hotel will only set aside a limited number of rooms for you (usually a maximum of 10), and then set a booking deadline. Any rooms not booked by your guests before the deadline will go back into regular circulation and can be booked by the general public.

If all 10 of your courtesy block rooms are booked before the deadline, you might be able to add additional rooms to your block, subject to availability and hotel policy. Inquire about this at the time you set up your room block.

For this reason, it can be a good idea to set up courtesy blocks at more than one hotel. This gives your guests options, but it also ensures that you will have enough rooms available for booking.

Choose king or queen bedded rooms

I recommend doing a mix: half the rooms with one king bed in them, and the other half with two queen beds. Again, this gives your guests more options. For people traveling with kids, or friends who want to share a room, having the option of reserving a room with two beds will be helpful.

Find out the discounted rate

Hotels sometimes offer you a discounted rate when they set up a room block for you, even for a courtesy block. But the discount may not be that significant. It's possible that a lower rate will be available through Internet promotions or travel websites. But for your guests who are less travel-savvy, it's nice to have the discounted room block rate available.

You also want to ask if there are any perks for you, like a complimentary night's stay. Many hotels will give you a free room the night of your wedding if your group books a certain number of rooms.

If you don't need a room the night of your wedding, find out if you can use the free room another time. Or maybe you want to use it the night before your wedding so that you have a room available for hair and makeup on your wedding day. Check-in time at most hotels is mid-afternoon, so if you need a spot for hair and makeup, you'll have to reserve the room for the previous night.

Get the codes to share with your guests

Most hotels will give you a website link that you can post directly on your wedding website. When your guests click the link, it takes them to a special reservations portal where the discount is already applied, and the computer knows that the reservation belongs with your group.

For guests who prefer to book their hotel over the phone, you will also be given a group code (usually some combination of the couple's last names) that they can provide to a reservations agent when calling to make their reservation.

Share the information

Encourage your guests to book their rooms early so that the room block doesn't fill up. If you live in a popular destination, you'll want to set up your room block before you send out your save-the-date cards. When guests go to your wedding website (listed on your save-the-dates), they'll want to see travel information and start making plans.

Your Homework Assignment

Decide whether you have enough out-of-town guests to warrant arranging hotel room blocks. If so, follow the steps above.

Transportation

When planning your wedding, it's easy to get caught up in the fun, pretty details like florals and gowns and favors. But don't forget about the important logistics, like how you're getting to and from your own wedding. Here's what you need to know about wedding transportation.

For the Couple

You and your fiancé(e) will not be arriving at the wedding venue together, but you will be leaving together. Having a plan in place will save you a lot of headaches. Lucky for you, these days there are abundant transportation options.

If you're getting married in a city (or at least not too far out into the countryside), Lyft and Uber are the most convenient options. You don't have to worry about stashing a car anywhere, and you don't have to worry about driving after drinking all night at your wedding. This is also super helpful if you plan to make multiple stops — say, the after-party, followed by your hotel. Maybe your wedding night is a good time to splurge on an Uber Black car.

If you want to depart in style, considering hiring a luxury auto, such as a Rolls Royce, Bentley, or Maserati. If you're planning a grand exit, stepping out and into the waiting car is a fabulous photo op. You can hire the car to arrive just before the end of your reception.

If you're holding your ceremony in a church or other religious institution, it can make sense to have a luxury car or limo bring you to the ceremony location, wait during the ceremony, and then drive you and your new spouse to the reception location. But financially, it does not make sense to have a luxury car sitting at your reception location for the rest of the evening until you leave, so keep that in mind.

For the Wedding Party

Depending on how large your wedding party is, you may want to arrange a limousine to drop everyone off at the wedding venue and then pick them up again at the end of the night. This only works if all wedding party members are going back to the same place — like a hotel or the after-party. If your wedding party is very large, you can rent a shuttle instead of a limo.

Group wedding party transportation is especially helpful if your wedding is in a remote location where Lyft and Uber are less likely to operate, or if you're concerned about wedding party members showing up late. (Granted, they might still miss the shuttle if they are notoriously tardy, but having pre-arranged transportation makes it more likely that they will arrive on time.)

For the Wedding Guests

If many of your guests are coming in from out of town and staying in hotels, it's a nice touch to have group transportation lined up. You (or your wedding planner) can arrange for shuttle buses to make stops at each hotel where you have reserved group room blocks. This requires careful coordination of timing to make sure there's sufficient time to stop at all hotels, wait several minutes for stragglers, and get to the wedding venue.

It's possible to have multiple buses lined up to make multiple trips, or if your venue is close enough to the venue, one shuttle can make a run and then go back to the hotels for a second run. In lieu of shuttle buses, other fun options include school buses or street cars/trolleys.

If you are not providing group transportation for your wedding guests, you should let them know in advance what the parking options at the venue are like—whether there's valet parking or self-parking, whether there's a parking lot or street parking. Your wedding website is a great place for this information, as are your welcome gift bags.

If you want to provide guest transportation without the hassle of setting up shuttles, Lyft and Uber have the ability to set up an event code. Your guests use the code when they request their ride at the end of the night, and the ride is charged to you. Simple!

Cost

Keep in mind that shuttle buses can be rather expensive. You'll need to budget at least $1000. The costs increase as you add shuttles or trips. The cost for individual cars is less, but there is generally a minimum number of hours, so it's best to think through how you can maximize the time to get your money's worth.

Here are some tips to keep in mind when you're searching for limousine, party bus, or car service.

Inquire about wedding packages

Many transportation companies offer savings on wedding packages since they require fewer hours than a standard rental. It can even come with added features such as decorations and beverages for extra convenience.

Do they have experience with your venue?

Asking if potential limousine and party bus services have experience with your specific venue will help narrow down the selection. A reputable company knows the city well enough so this isn't a problem regardless, but it's an advantage to book with a service who knows the small details about your specific venue. This is especially true if your venue is hard to find or in an area without cell phone coverage. The last thing you want is the shuttle getting lost with no way to contact anyone for help with directions.

Are you allowed to view your vehicle in person?

Inquire about scheduling a visit to the company to ensure that everything is as luxurious as it seems on the website. This is especially true for classic cars. Those cars are by definition old, and up-close they may have flaws that aren't apparent in photos.

Your Homework Assignment

Decide who needs transportation. Begin making inquiries and getting quotes. Transportation companies are notoriously bad at customer service. You may have to follow up multiple times to get anyone to give you a quote. Sad but true.

Toasting

Toasts are a traditional part of a wedding. Usually, the Maid of Honor and Best Man each offers a toast. Often, the father (or parents) of the bride (or groom) does as well.

You might be tempted to allow others to make a toast, but those are better left for the rehearsal dinner, where more speaking is expected. At a wedding, people expect to eat, drink, and dance.

Here's some advice to share with those who will be giving toasts to prevent them from derailing your wedding day.

1. Keep it short

No toast should last more than 5 minutes. The best are between 3 and 4 minutes. Regardless of how witty the toaster thinks they are, your guests really don't care that much. (It sounds harsh, but it's true.)

2. Keep it relevant

Please don't be like the maid of honor at one wedding who recounted seemingly every single moment she and the bride had shared growing up. Again, no one really cares. A brief description of your relationship to the couple is sufficient. The toast should primarily be about the couple, not about your escapades with one half of the couple.

3. Make it heartfelt

Wedding toasts aren't the time to make jokes at the expense of the couple. It's a toast, not a roast. A toast can be funny, but it should also be sincere and kind. It should be about how well-suited for each other the couple are. It should be about how happy you are for them, and how happy they make each other. It's their wedding day, not open-mic night.

4. Write it down

The only thing worse than a long toast is a rambling toast. Prepare your remarks in advance, and practice them out loud while timing yourself (see tip #1). Memorize your toast if you can, but always have a written back up copy with you at the wedding.

5. Finish with an actual toast

A toast isn't just your opportunity to wax poetic in front of a crowd. It serves a specific purpose: you are wishing the couple happiness in their married life. At the end, you should ask everyone to raise a glass to the couple. And don't forget to take your glass with you when you go up to make your toast, so you can raise your glass as well.

If you follow these tips, you will give a successful toast, and no one will remember you as "that guy who rambled on incoherently for 10 minutes." That's a worthy goal!

Your Homework Assignment

Decide who will give toasts at your wedding. Confirm with those people that they want to give a toast. Send them this chapter. Remind them repeatedly to keep their toast under 5 minutes.

Bouquet and Garter Toss

Are you planning a bouquet or garter toss for your wedding? Not sure whether you want to? You're not alone. A somewhat surprising number of my clients ask me what I think about doing a bouquet or garter toss. The answer, as with most wedding-related traditions, is that it's a matter of personal preference.

I haven't done the math on this, but anecdotally, I would say that about half my clients opt to do both a bouquet and a garter toss. About three-quarters do at least the bouquet toss, and around a quarter of couples don't do either.

Traditionally, these tosses were meant to be a way for some of the wedding couple's good luck to rub off on the guests. The people who caught the bouquet and garter were supposedly going to be the next to get married. This is why only single/unmarried people are typically called out to the dance floor for the bouquet and garter toss.

This is something to keep in mind when weighing whether or not to do a toss: how many single friends and relatives do you have? If the answer is "not many," you might want to skip this tradition. The fun of it comes from getting a large crowd out onto the dance floor, and maybe some good-natured jostling to be the one to catch the bouquet or garter. With just a few people out there, it's less of a spectacle.

But if you do have mostly married friends and still want to do a bouquet and garter toss, just let your DJ know that you want to include all guests, not just the single ones. That way you still get the fun of the activity without calling out your single friends. Because let's be honest, it's a little awkward for someone to call attention to the fact that they are unmarried by going out to the floor for the bouquet toss.

Plus, what does "single" even mean? Lots of people are unmarried but not single. Phrasing is really important when it comes to the bouquet and garter toss.

Bouquet toss

If you decide to do a bouquet toss, ask your florist to make you a small "tossing" bouquet. You might want to save your actual bouquet. Maybe you plan to have it preserved intact, or maybe you're going to dismantle it and have individual stems pressed as a keepsake. You won't be able to do this if you give away your bouquet. Bridal bouquets are also heavy. A small tossing bouquet is easier to toss, easier to catch, and safer.

Garter toss

Etsy is a great place to find garters. Many of them come in sets of two so you can toss one and keep the other as a memento. And if you get a blue garter, you've wrapped up your "something new," "something blue," and your garter all at once. Wedding multitasking, for the win!

Your Homework Assignment

Decide whether you want to do the bouquet and garter toss, just the bouquet, or neither. Choose songs for the appropriate toss. Some DJs recommend two songs for each toss—one song while they call people out onto the dance floor and a second song for the actual toss. It's up to you!

Ring Care

Your engagement and wedding rings are a significant financial and emotional investment. Here's how to treat them with the respect they deserve.

Insurance

You insure your house, your car, and your life. Why wouldn't you also insure the thousands of dollars worth of jewelry that you are now wearing on a regular basis? Jewelry insurance is easy to come by and reasonably priced. If you already have a homeowner's or renter's policy, you can add a jewelry rider to it or obtain a separate personal articles policy.

You'll need an appraisal with a detailed description of the rings and a current value. If you've been walking around for years with an uninsured engagement ring, not to worry. Any jeweler can provide an appraisal for a small fee.

Insuring your rings protects you if your rings are lost, stolen, or damaged. You want to be sure to insure them for "replacement value," so that if they are lost or stolen, you can get a replacement ring of the same specifications.

I recommend obtaining insurance as soon as you take delivery of the rings. Don't wait until after the wedding or honeymoon. You never know what could happen.

Exercise & Water sports

Never wear your wedding rings while exercising. It's potentially dangerous for both you and the ring. Your fingers swell during exercise. It's possible for your fingers to swell so much that your ring cuts off circulation to your finger. Gangrene is not a good look on anyone.

Your ring is also much more likely to be lost or damaged if you wear it during exercise. Hitting the weight room? Careful not to bang your hand into anything. Stand-up paddle boarding? Good luck retrieving your ring from the bottom of the lake. Play it safe and remove all jewelry before exercise.

Sleeping & Bathing

Along the same lines, rings should be removed before sleeping or bathing. Rings can easily slide off of wet fingers, and I don't think you want to be fishing your engagement ring out of the shower drain.

And much like exercising, you should be sleeping without jewelry. As with exercise, your fingers can swell during sleep. Plus, it's good to give your skin a break from being in contact with metal.

Cleaning & Gardening

Have you started to notice a trend here yet? Basically, any time you're doing any activity that could potentially damage your rings, you should remove them. If you wear gardening gloves or rubber gloves while cleaning, then it's okay to wear your rings because they will be protected. But you should remove them before doing anything with your bare hands.

Maintenance & Care

Have your ring professionally cleaned once a year, and while it's "in the shop" have a jeweler inspect it for damage. That could include tiny knicks, loose prongs or settings, or scratches. Clean your ring periodically at home as well, either with a professional jewelry cleaner or with a little dish soap and warm water. Just remember to plug the sink before cleaning!

With proper care, your rings will last a lifetime.

Your Homework Assignment

Get insurance for your ring. Right now. I'm not kidding. You can do this online. Also insure your wedding bands as soon as you get them.

Wedding Insurance

Clients sometimes ask me about wedding insurance: what it is, how to get it, and whether they need it. Much like all other insurance policies, you don't really need it, until you do.

Many venues require couples to obtain wedding liability insurance, also known as special event coverage. But even if your venue doesn't require it, having insurance is never a bad idea. Insurance protects the venue and the hosts from liability in the event of an accident—someone slips on the dance floor and breaks their leg, someone gets drunk and causes property damage, an errant candle catches the drapes on fire. Your typical nightmare scenarios.

Wedding insurance is fairly easy and inexpensive to obtain. If the host (either the couple or one set of parents) has a homeowner's insurance policy, they can talk with their agent about a temporary rider that can be added to the policy for the event. If that's not an option, there are companies that specialize in event insurance.

WedSafe, WedSure, and even Progressive all provide special event liability insurance. These companies also provide wedding cancellation insurance to cover your deposits (which can be substantial) in the unfortunate event that you need to postpone or cancel your wedding. Most couples didn't consider this to be a real possibility, until the COVID-19 pandemic. That illustrates better than any hypothetical I could ever dream up why investing in cancellation insurance is a good idea.

The pandemic also prompted a lot of insurance companies to specifically exclude future pandemics from "covered events," which is insurance-speak meaning, "This policy is useless in the event of a global pandemic." So when researching policies, you'll want to carefully read the "exclusions" section and call the company to verify coverage if it's unclear.

The good news though is that the cost of wedding insurance is reasonable. For just a few hundred dollars, you can get hundreds of thousands of dollars worth of coverage. In the end, it's worth it for the peace of mind it provides. As the old adage goes, better safe than sorry.

Your Homework Assignment

Check your venue contract to see what amount of insurance is required. If the contract doesn't specify, use $1 million to be safe. Research policies using the websites listed above. Decide whether you want liability insurance only or if you also want cancellation insurance.

Do not skip insurance. You don't have to get full cancellation coverage, but liability insurance is a must, even if your venue doesn't require it.

Tipping Your Wedding Team

One of the questions I'm asked most often is how much to tip various wedding professionals. There are no hard-and-fast rules on this, but there are some guidelines to help you make your tipping decisions. As with all gratuities, they are discretionary. If you feel like your wedding team members served you well and provided good or excellent service, feel free to tip accordingly. If you feel that they did not live up to expectations, you are within your rights to not offer a gratuity.

Hair & Makeup Professionals

This category is pretty easy because most of us are used to tipping our hairstylist when we go to the salon. The standard 15-20% guidance applies to wedding hair and makeup professionals as well. Keep in mind that if you (as the bride) are paying for your wedding party's hair and makeup services, you should also budget for those additional gratuities.

Delivery People

It is customary to tip non-owner delivery people $5-10 cash. If flowers or the cake are delivered by someone other than the business owner, it's nice to give them a little something. Typically, you as the couple will not be the ones taking delivery because you're busy getting ready. But it's easy enough to provide cash ahead of time to whomever will be taking delivery, whether it's your wedding planner or coordinator or a family member or friend.

Creative Professionals

Here's where things start to get a little more complicated. For pros such as your planner/coordinator, florist, DJ, photographer, or videographer, it depends on whether they own their own business or work for someone else.

Business owners set their own pricing, and they generally charge what they believe is a fair price for their services. Gratuities are not expected. That said, everyone loves being rewarded for a job well done. If you feel that your creative wedding pros went above and beyond your expectations and delivered exceptional service, a little extra gratuity will always be appreciated. You can even send it after the fact — it doesn't have to be something you have with you at the wedding.

If you decide to tip these creative professionals, a guideline amount is 10-20% of their total fee, or $100-250, depending on your overall budget and how grateful you are for their services.

For service providers who do not own the business—think of a DJ who works for a larger entertainment company or a second shooter working for a photographer—$50-$150 is a good benchmark. This should be given as cash at the end of the wedding, rather than delivered later, because you may not have a way to reach them later.

Bartenders

Bartenders start to get even trickier because some of them put out tip jars on the bar. I frown on this practice, and discourage my clients from allowing a tip jar to be put out. You are hosting an event for your guests; they shouldn't be expected to contribute financially to the event. Just as it's inappropriate to ask your guests to pay for drinks, it's equally inappropriate to ask your guests to tip the bartenders.

That said, if your bartenders do put out a tip jar, you should not add any additional gratuity on top of that. But if they do not put out a tip jar, $50-100 per bartender is customary. (Some bar service companies will spell out in their contract how much each bartender must be tipped in lieu of a tip jar. Again, I find this gauche, and I tend not to do business with those bar services if I find out that's their practice.)

Catering & Service Staff

This is the most complicated category, and somewhat depends on whether the service staff are employed/provided by the caterers or hired separately.

If the catering company provides all the staff, the easiest way to calculate the tip is to take 10-20% of the total catering bill and give a lump sum amount (either cash or check) to the catering or sales manager to be distributed after the wedding. If you are paying cash, a variety of small bills ($5, $10, and $20 bills) is easiest to divvy up.

If you would prefer to tip individually, you can find out from the catering manager ahead of time how many service staff they will be bringing and prepare tip envelopes ahead of time. Customary amounts are $50-100 for the catering manager, chef, or carving chef and $20-30 per server.

When service staff is hired separately from the caterer—for example, if a restaurant is catering but does not provide the staff—these individual guidelines are also applicable.

One thing to remember is that the "service fee" charged by catering companies is almost never a gratuity that goes to the staff. The service fee is usually an amount 18-22% of the total catering bill that the company uses to cover overhead and other costs of doing business. Although it sounds like a fee for the service staff, it is not. We covered this in-depth back in the "caterer and bar service" section of Chapter 4.

One last tip (no pun intended): any gratuity envelopes that you've prepared in advance can be given to your wedding planner/coordinator early in the day so she can distribute them to the appropriate people at the appropriate time. Some team members leave before the end of the reception, and you don't want to be interrupted on the dance floor to have to track down a tip envelope that you stashed somewhere earlier in the night. And once the party's over, you will still be busy, saying goodbye to friends or heading to your after-party. These sort of logistical details are best left to your planner.

Your Homework Assignment

Make a list of all your wedding team members. Using the guidance above, decide which ones you intend to tip and write an amount next to their name. Get cash from the bank, put it in separate envelopes (with or without a little note). Ask your wedding coordinator or a trusted wedding party member to distribute the tips at the appropriate time.

Remember, you can always send a note and a tip after the wedding if you feel like you got exceptional service from someone but didn't plan ahead to tip them.

Time to Celebrate!

You did it! You made it to the end, and your wedding should be well in hand at this point. If you followed all of the homework assignments, here's what you've accomplished:

- You created a wedding budget and guest list, and chose your wedding party members.
- You decided on a date, location, and aesthetic for your wedding.
- You booked a venue and hired all of the wedding professionals who will make your day a joyous one to remember, including a coordinator to make sure everything runs smoothly on your big day.
- You set up your wedding website, complete with registry information and hotel and transportation information, if applicable.
- You've got attire worked out for yourselves and your wedding party, and gifts for your spouse, wedding party, and parents
- You know which little wedding details you want to order and have a good idea of where to get them.
- You know how to handle ordering invitations, and when to send them.
- You're ready to figure out your seating chart once all of your RSVPs come in.
- You've got all the necessary insurance and are ready to rock and roll on your wedding day!

I sincerely hope this book was helpful to you and has allowed you to avoid some of the overwhelming stress that comes with planning a wedding. I want you to have a beautiful, relaxing wedding day, and a truly happy married life!

CHAPTER 6

Questionnaires

Bakery Questionnaire

Company Name

Contact Name

Email/phone number

Website/Instagram

Available on our date(s)?

Do you have a minimum order amount?

Do you charge for delivery?

Is there a travel fee?

Payment options and schedule?

Do you include a complimentary anniversary cake?

How many flavors can we try at our tasting?

Is there a tasting fee?

Will you make sheet cakes in addition to our cutting cake?

Do you make desserts other than cakes?

Will you place our floral cake décor on our cake?

Will anything need to be returned to you?

Do you pick up those items or do we have to return them?

Do you specialize in anything in particular?

Do you offer any rental or décor items?

Notes.

Bar Service Questionnaire

Company Name

Contact Name

Email/phone number

Website/Instagram

Available on our date(s)?

How many weddings do you do per year/per weekend?

How many bartenders do you recommend for our wedding?

Can you create custom signature cocktails for us?

Do you provide alcohol, mixers, and garnishes?

Do you provide ice?

If we provide the alcohol and other ingredients, will you tell us how much to buy?

Will you pour wine tableside during dinner?

Do you have any discounts for purchasing wine or spirits vs. us purchasing them ourselves?

Do you offer vegan/allergen-free options?

Do you offer locally sourced and sustainable ingredients?

Do you provide glassware or do you manage the rental of those items?

Are you fully licensed for liquor service?

Are you insured? What kind of coverage?

What happens if you are unable to attend our wedding?

Do you have a travel fee?

Payment options and schedule?

Notes.

Calligrapher Questionnaire

Company Name

Contact Name

Email/phone number

Website/Instagram

Available on our date(s)?

Do you have a minimum order amount?

Do you charge for delivery?

How much lead time do you need?

Do you provide easels for signage?

Do you have any rental items or is everything custom?

Do you have different styles of calligraphy?

Do we need to provide the supplies for escort and place cards?

How many ink colors can we choose from?

What if our invitation envelopes are damaged in your care?

Do you have liability insurance?

Will anything need to be returned to you?

Do you pick up those items or do we have to return them?

What materials do you recommend for our wedding style?

Payment options and schedule?

Notes.

Caterer Questionnaire

Company Name

Contact Name

Email/phone number

Website/Instagram

Available on our date(s)?

How many weddings do you do per year/per weekend?

Do you have pre-set menus or can we create one from scratch?

Do you provide waitstaff and bussers?

Does your staff place linens, plates, glasses, silverware, etc.?

Do you also offer appetizers, desserts, and/or bar service?

What is the tasting fee? Is it applied to our final order?

How many options can we try at the tasting?

Do tastings happen at pre-determined times or can we schedule one when it's convenient for us?

Do you offer vegan/vegetarian/allergen-free options?

Do you offer locally sourced and sustainable ingredients?

Do you provide linens, plates, glasses, etc., or do you manage the rental of those items?

Are you fully licensed for food service and/or liquor service?

Are you insured? What kind of coverage?

What happens if you are unable to attend our wedding?

Do you have a travel fee?

Payment options and schedule?

Notes.

Ceremony Musicians Questionnaire

Company Name

Contact Name

Email/phone number

Website/Instagram

Available on our date(s)?

How many weddings do you book per weekend?

What is your minimum number of hours?

Do we need to provide sheet music?

Do you charge extra for a separate cocktail hour set-up?

Do we need to provide chairs or anything else?

Can we see photos of your usual set-up?

Do you specialize in a particular genre?

Are there any limitations on the type of music you play?

Do you require breaks? How many and how long?

Are you insured? What kind of coverage?

What happens if you are unable to attend our wedding?

Do you have a travel fee?

Payment options and schedule?

Notes.

Coordinator Questionnaire

Company Name

Contact Name

Email/phone number

Website/Instagram

Available on our date(s)?

How many weddings do you do per year/per weekend?

Will you be our actual coordinator at our wedding?

Will you have any assistants?

How long before the wedding will we start working together?

How many hours will you be on-site at our wedding?

Do you charge extra if our ceremony is not in the same location as the reception?

Do you handle decorating the space?

Can you relocate décor from the ceremony to the reception?

Do you prepare a timeline and floor plans?

Do you submit weddings for publication?

Do you have a partial planning service?

Will you be present at our ceremony rehearsal?

Are you insured? What kind of coverage?

What happens if you are unable to attend our wedding?

Do you have a travel fee?

Payment options and schedule?

Notes.

Décor Questionnaire

Company Name

Contact Name

Email/phone number

Website/Instagram

Available on our date(s)?

Do you have a minimum order amount?

Do you charge for delivery and set-up?

Will you deliver and set-up in multiple locations?

Do you provide all the items from inventory or will you manage a rental order for us?

Do you handle tent draping, pipe & drape, stage decoration, etc.?

When do you come back to the venue to take down décor?

Will you relocate décor from the ceremony site to the reception site during cocktail hour?

Do you offer any lighting options, including chandeliers?

Do you have lounge furniture, ceremony arches, and/or heaters?

Are you familiar with our venue?

What happens if items are damaged during the wedding?

Are you insured? What kind of coverage?

What happens if you are unable to attend our wedding?

Do you have a travel fee?

Payment options and schedule?

Notes.

DJ/Band Questionnaire

Company Name

Contact Name

Email/phone number

Website/Instagram

Available on our date(s)?

How many weddings do you do per year/per weekend?

Will you be our actual DJ/MC at our wedding?

Do you provide lighting? What types?

Do you offer a photo booth or other services?

Do you charge extra for a separate ceremony set-up?

How many and what type of microphones are provided?

Can we see photos of your usual set-up?

Do you specialize in a particular genre?

How do you handle song requests from guests?

Can we submit "must play" and "do not play" lists?

Do you mix beats or just play songs in succession?

Do you read the dance floor and change things up?

Do you require breaks? How many and how long?

Are you insured? What kind of coverage?

What happens if you are unable to attend our wedding?

Do you have a travel fee?

Payment options and schedule?

Notes.

Florist Questionnaire

Company Name

Contact Name

Email/phone number

Website/Instagram

Available on our date(s)?

Do you have a minimum order amount?

Do you charge for delivery and set-up?

Will you deliver and set-up in multiple locations?

Do you include a complimentary toss bouquet?

Will you make a centerpiece mock-up for approval?

Can you provide extra loose stems on the wedding day?

How far in advance do you make the arrangements?

Where do you source your flowers?

How many weddings per day do you service?

Will anything need to be returned to you?

Do you pick up those items or do we have to return them?

Is there any floral element you won't work with?

Do you offer any rental or décor items?

Are you insured? What kind of coverage?

What happens if you are unable to attend our wedding?

Payment options and schedule?

Notes.

Hair & Makeup Questionnaire

Company Name

Contact Name

Email/phone number

Website/Instagram

Available on our date(s)?

Do you have a minimum fee or number of hours?

Do you offer both hair and makeup?

Do you work with any assistants? How many do you recommend for my wedding party?

Will you come to us or do we have to come to your salon?

How much time should I budget for my hair and makeup and the bridesmaids/ mothers hair and makeup?

Will you place my hair décor/veil?

Do you use vegan/cruelty-free products?

Do you airbrush or offer any other special techniques?

When should I schedule a hair and makeup trial?

What is the fee for a trial?

Are you licensed and insured?

What happens if you are unable to attend our wedding?

Do you have a travel fee?

Payment options and schedule?

Notes.

Officiant Questionnaire

Company Name

Contact Name

Email/phone number

Website/Instagram

Available on our date(s)?

How many ceremonies do you book per day?

Do you have sample ceremonies we can see?

Will you work with us to incorporate personal touches?

Do you mail in our paperwork after the wedding?

Are you comfortable with different cultural traditions?

Are you bi-lingual? (if applicable)

Do you offer or require any pre-marital counseling?

How far in advance do you need our personal vows?

Will you attend our ceremony rehearsal?

What happens if you are unable to attend our wedding?

Do you have a travel fee?

Payment options and schedule?

Notes.

Photographer Questionnaire

Company Name

Contact Name

Email/phone number

Website/Instagram

Available on our date(s)?

How many weddings do you do per year/per weekend?

Will you be our actual photographer at our wedding?

How many photographers will cover our wedding?

Approximately how many images do you typically deliver for a wedding of our size/length of service package?

How long after the wedding will we receive our photos?

Do you send any "sneak peeks" right after the wedding?

Do you offer wedding albums?

How do you deliver the final images?

Do you submit weddings for publication?

Do you offer engagement photo sessions?

Do you offer a photo booth or other services?

Do you do any retouching?

Are you insured? What kind of coverage?

What happens if you are unable to attend our wedding?

Do you have a travel fee?

Payment options and schedule?

Notes.

Rental/Tent Questionnaire

Company Name

Contact Name

Email/phone number

Website/Instagram

Available on our date(s)? (Mainly applies to tents.)

Do you have a minimum order amount?

What is the charge for delivery and set-up?

Will you deliver and set-up in multiple locations?

Do you provide all the items from inventory or will you manage a rental order for us?

What special policies apply to tent rentals?

Do you handle tent draping, pipe & drape, stage decoration, etc.?

When do you come back to the venue to dismantle the tent/pick up rental items?

Will you relocate ceremony chairs from the ceremony site to the reception site during cocktail hour?

Do you offer any lighting options, including chandeliers?

Do you have lounge furniture, ceremony arches, and/or heaters?

Are you familiar with our venue?

Will you do a site visit to evaluate the property for a tent?

When do we have to finalize our order?

What happens if items are damaged during the wedding?

Payment options and schedule?

Notes.

Venue Questionnaire

Company Name

Contact Name

Email/phone number

Website/Instagram

Available on our date(s)?

Guest capacity or minimum?

Rental fee?

What's included in the fee?

Payment options and schedule?

Exclusive use of property?

Length of rental (days or hours)?

Noise restrictions/end time of event?

Can we bring in our own caterer and/or alcohol?

Is there a full kitchen on-site?

Can we use service providers not on your preferred list?

Is there space to get ready?

Are there any décor restrictions?

When can our rehearsal take place?

Notes.

Videographer Questionnaire

Company Name

Contact Name

Email/phone number

Website/Instagram

Available on our date(s)?

How many weddings do you do per year/per weekend?

Will you be our actual videographer at our wedding?

How many videographers will cover our wedding?

How long will the final edited video be?

How long after the wedding will we receive our video?

Do we get the raw footage or only the edited video?

Do we get any input into the music used in the final video?

Do you offer a shorter "social media" edit?

What types of camera set-ups do you use? Tripods, gimbals, etc.?

Do you shoot any drone footage?

Do you offer a photo booth or other services?

Do you do any retouching?

How do you deliver the final video?

Are you insured? What kind of coverage?

What happens if you are unable to attend our wedding?

Do you have a travel fee?

Payment options and schedule?

Notes.

Index

S

Seating chart 9, 17, 26, 61
Signage 9, 26, 44, 94, 142, 144
Skincare 129
Sustainability 25

T

Table assignments 27
Tablecloths 157, 158
Templates 3
Tents 201
Theme 53, 114
Tipping 173

Toasts 166
Transportation 33, 163, 165

V

Venue 8, 30, 43, 44, 45, 46, 203
Videographer 74, 75, 205
Videography 8, 9

W

Wedding blog 1
Wedding party 16, 20
Wedding website 4, 18, 52

About the Author

Risa Weaver-Enion is a wedding planner based in Sacramento, CA. A life-long writer, when she launched her wedding planning business in 2015, she immediately started blogging with helpful tips for engaged couples. After writing nearly 100 blog posts, she realized that her knowledge and experience would serve more couples in book form.

Since launching Risa James Events, Risa has guided nearly 70 couples through the wedding planning process. Her attention to detail, grace under pressure, and ability to execute complicated weddings has led to her winning WeddingWire's Couples' Choice Award for five consecutive years. Her advice has been featured in multiple publications, including Upjourney.com, Shefinds.com, Honeyfund.com, and *Long Island Bride & Groom*.

Risa holds a bachelor's degree in history from Case Western Reserve University in Cleveland, and a *juris doctor* from Duke University School of Law in Durham, North Carolina. She has no hesitation in proclaiming that being a wedding planner is much more fun than being an attorney.

She lives in West Sacramento, California with the love of her life, her husband Rhead. When she's not writing or planning weddings, you can find her making and photographing craft cocktails or visiting wineries and distilleries around the world.

For more information about planning a wedding, including guest blog posts not included in this book, visit www.risajamesevents.com.

To keep up with Risa on Instagram, find her wedding work @risajamesevents and her cocktail photography @risajamesphotography.

If you have questions for Risa, you can reach her via email at risa@risajamesevents.com.

Made in the USA
Middletown, DE
30 December 2021

57303028R00130